# ROCKBAND™

## PRIMA Official Game Guide
### Damien Waples

Prima Games
A Division of Random House, Inc.
3000 Lava Ridge Court, Suite 100
Roseville, CA 95661

www.primagames.com

Damien grew up wishing he could play the guitar like Dave Mustaine and the bass like Steve Harris (okay, he still wishes), but the only thing "metal" that he ever really accomplished was growing a pretty kick-ass mullet in high school.

He has authored or co-authored over 30 game guides and has earned a masters in business administration from Sacramento State University, where he also taught. He enjoys playing ice hockey and air guitar (not at the same time) and hanging out with his favorite little rockers—his nephews Trevor and Tristan.

We want to hear from you! E-mail comments and feedback to dwaples@primagames.com.

Senior Product Manager: Donato Tica
Editor: Rebecca Chastain
Copyeditor: Carrie Andrews
Design: Calibre Grafix, LLC
Layout: James Knight
Manufacturing: Stephanie Sanchez

**Important:**
Prima Games has made every effort to determine that the information contained in this book is accurate. However, the publisher makes no warranty, either expressed or implied, as to the accuracy, effectiveness, or completeness of the material in this book; nor does the publisher assume liability for damages, either incidental or consequential, that may result from using the information in this book. The publisher cannot provide any additional information or support regarding gameplay, hints and strategies, or problems with hardware or software. Such questions should be directed to the support numbers provided by the game and/or device manufacturers as set forth in their documentation. Some game tricks require precise timing and may require repeated attempts before the desired result is achieved.

ISBN: 978-0-7615-5882-8
Library of Congress Catalog Card Number: 200794350
Printed in the United States of America

07 08 09 10 GG 10 9 8 7 6 5 4 3 2 1

# ROCKBAND

# TABLE OF CONTENTS

\* This is a cover version of a song made famous by the artist indicated.

# INTRODUCTION

Honestly, this is one of the most entertaining projects we've ever worked on and hopefully that comes through in the writing. You can't help but have fun playing through these songs with a group of friends. In fact, we really don't know how any writing got done at all! But fortunately it did, and we hope you enjoy what we've come up with, even half as much as we enjoyed coming up with it.

Very special thanks go to Dan Teasdale at Harmonix, for all of his help and support throughout the project. Prima would also like to thank Kris Fell, Aaron Price, Spencer Saltonstall, Keith Smith, Justin Stanizzi, and Grace Williams for their invaluable insight and assistance. Finally, we'd like to express our gratitude to Peter Banks at MTV games. It was a pleasure working with all of you!

Turn it up!
**Damien Waples**

# TOURING AND TRAINING

We're gonna let the instruction manual fill you in on the basics so we can focus on helping you make the most of your Rock Band experience. To do so, we need to concentrate on three areas: Solo Tour mode, Band World Tour mode, and Training.

# SOLO TOUR

In Solo Tour mode, you work your way form obscurity to stardom, earning money and fame along the way.

The first thing you need to do is create a new rocker. Select "Create New" from the "Select Rocker" screen and proceed through the process to customize your avatar. Make sure you alter his or her attitude and physique to best fit your taste.

Once you've created your rocker, you are taken to the Solo Tour menu screen (Screen Shot 1.1). Here you can visit the Rock Shop, play a gig, view your profile and visit the leaderboards.

Screen Shot 1.1: Solo Tour menu

You'll definitely want to check out the Rock Shop. Here you can buy clothing and equipment, purchase different haircuts, design tattoos and apply make-up and face paint.

There are near infinite possibilities in terms of character customization. The folks at Harmonix have created bands consisting of super-heroes, gaming icons, and even Ronald McDonald! Keith Smith, the Quality Assurance Lead, even re-created the original Sex pistols lineup.

3

# ROCKBAND™

Select "Play Gig" to begin your tour. In order to play all 58 songs, you must choose Medium, Hard, or Expert difficulty (easy difficulty contains only 43 songs). If you are new to the game, we would suggest starting with Medium. It might be tough at first, but better that than choosing Easy and then 20 songs into the tour you find you are no longer challenged. And remember, if you find yourself struggling, you can always practice the parts of the song that are causing you problems (from the main menu, select "Training", then "Practice Mode").

**Screen Shot 1.2: Solo Tour song selection**

The Solo Tour song selection screen includes all of the songs and venues that you've unlocked. When you begin for the first time, the first five songs are available. You can play them in any order, but you must complete all five in order to open up the next venue and song list.

Songs get harder in difficulty as you progress.

Once you complete a song, the "New" label is replaced with a star rating and a score. The money you earn is directly related to the number of stars you earn, so the higher you score, the richer you become. If you are unhappy with your score, you can replay the song as many times as you like.

Aside from the five songs that are available right away, you can visit Rio de Janeiro and play the Bonus Tour. While there, every song you complete opens up an additional song. Be aware that the songs in Rio are more difficult than many of the songs in the Solo Tour.

Completing the Bonus Tour is not required to finish the Solo Tour, however, a special instrument is unlocked if you do.

That's all you need to know to get you up and playing the Solo Tour, except that completing it unlocks a new instrument (different than the Bonus Tour item). Also, as you complete songs in either the Solo Tour or Band World Tour modes, the songs become available in Practice mode.

# MULTIPLAYER

There are four options within the Multiplayer menu: Band Quickplay, Band World Tour, Tug of War, and Score Duel. Band Quickplay is very similar to Solo Quickplay, except that you play with other people. Select this option when you want to rock out to a favorite song without affecting your World Tour stats.

Tug of war allows you to take on another player, using the same instrument, in a tug-of-war type contest. Players trade phrases, each trying to outdo the other and gain the advantage. Pull far enough ahead and you win.

The goal of Score Duel, as the name implies, is to outscore your opponent as you both play identical tracks. It's not all about fancy playing though, as a less skilled opponent with a superior grasp of overdrive can prevail.

## BAND WORLD TOUR

Band World Tour is the heart of Rock Band. It allows you start a band and hit the road, earning money, fans, and fame along the way.

The first step on your road to super-stardom is to create a band (and the award for pointing out the obvious goes to…). Select "Start a Band" from the Select Your Band screen to begin the process. Follow the onscreen prompts to select a name and a hometown.

People will get used to a bad name, assuming they like the music. You can even name your band after a vegetable (as long as you change the first letter).

Once you're ready to rock, select "Start Tour." One really important point: Your leader must always be present at a gig. Without him or her, you can't progress through the tour. However, you only need two members at any given time to play a gig (as long as one of them is the leader). The computer will fill in for any missing band members.

It's time to select your first song. The choices differ at each venue so here's a general rundown. You can select a single song to play or go for more fans and money by choosing either a multi-song set list or a mystery set list. If you select a set list, you play the specified number of songs all in a row. Fail one and you fail the gig. Failing a gig costs you fans, which will hinder you from progressing through the tour.

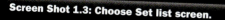

**Screen Shot 1.3: Choose Set list screen.**

5

# ROCKBAND™

Screen Shot 1.4: The Gig screen.

Screen Shot 1.4 shows the layout of the actual Gig screen. The vocal track runs along the top, the drums are in the center, and the guitar and bass are on either side of the drums track. The Crowd Meter is the vertical green bar on the far left side of the screen.

See the Instruments chapter for a discussion on the attributes of each instrument's music track. You'll need to know your instrument before you can contribute to a band.

The Crowd Meter and the score are affected by each band member's individual performance. For example, when the bassist kicks into overdrive, all members benefit, and the crowd responds in kind. Also, the score multipliers of each member stack. So, solid players that can keep a multiplier going are invaluable to a band.

There is a lot more to say, but sometimes it's best to defer to the experts. The next section contains tips to help you make the most out of the Band World Tour.

# ALL ACCESS

We sat down with the fine folks at Harmonix in order to bring you strategy straight from the people who know the game best.

## MEET THE DEVELOPERS

Aaron Price—Tester
Favorite songs to play:
"Welcome Home" on guitar,
"Flirtin' With Disaster" on Bass,
"Should I Stay or Should I Go"
on drums, and "Timmy and the
Lords of the Underworld" on
vocals.

**Keith Smith—Tester**
Favorite songs to play: "Welcome Home" for "epic" guitar playing, "Go With the Flow" for "chord fantasticness," and "Black Hole Sun" as a band.

**Justin Stanizzi—Tester**
Favorite songs to play: "Train Kept a Rollin'" and "Reptilia" on guitar, "Dani California" on bass, and "Won't Get Fooled Again" on drums.

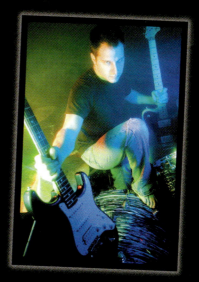

**Dan Teasdale—Senior Designer**
Favorite songs to play: "Run to the Hills" because "It's absolutely perfect for playing in *Rock Band*"; "Timmy and the Lords of the Underworld" because "Singing along is one of the most fun experiences you can possibly have in a video game"; and "Highway Star" on bass because "It's my personal hill to climb."

Grace Williams—Tester
Favorite songs to play:
"Green Grass and High Tides"
on expert guitar, "Dani
California" on Expert drums
and "Foreplay/Long Time" on
vocals.

## DRUM STRATEGY

Justin: "Learn to alternate
hands."

Grace: "Leave your foot resting on the
pedal. Bringing it all the way up and
then down again wears out your leg
fast."

Aaron: "Play the fills with a
constant rhythm because if you
just try and go wild and have fun,
you're gonna have a really hard
time getting back into the rhythm."

Keith: "If the kit is too high you'll be hitting rim
shots all the time, and not in the cool jazz way
but in the lame hit-the-controller way."

Dan: "By the time you're hitting
hard and expert, you'll definitely
have the skills to play drums in real
life."

## BASS STRATEGY

Aaron: "The bass is really important because it has the unique ability to get up to a 6x multiplier. If you're playing in a band, your multiplier applies to everybody else in the band. So if you have a bassist that's nice and steady, you're gonna help out the entire band."

Justin: "The bassist's 6x multiplier in conjunction with the exponential multipliers you get from all deploying overdrive at the same time will allow the band to reach five stars."

## GUITAR STRATEGY

Keith: "Use your overdrive wisely. For points, save it for long chord runs; for difficulty, save it for solos. There's nothing worse than owning in a song and then getting to a solo that backhands you down and causes you to fail quickly."

## VOCAL STRATEGY

Justin: "If you have a vocalist that is really into it and actually wants to sing out loud, even if they're not great at it, they'll tie the entire tune together and it just feels so much better.

Dan: "It really comes down to what you know. It's much easier to sing a song that you know, than learning on the fly."

Aaron: "Having a good time as a vocalist is a balance between being pitch accurate and actually letting go and having fun. If you don't care about scoring, select Easy, you won't fail out and it's basically like karaoke."

Grace: "It's not called 'lazy band' its called 'Rock Band' so rock out and have fun!"

## BIG ROCK ENDING STRATEGY

Keith: "The unofficial superstealth gansta way to go about it is to strum *while* using the high frets. It doubles your points."

Aaron: "There is a max number of points you can get per lane, so if you rapidly strum on one note, you'll max out on your points per second. However, if you rapidly strum up and down the fret board you'll get five times that amount. Move around rapidly and strum rapidly and that is gonna get you your max amount of points."

Grace: "Double-hand the high frets—one set of fingers playing regularly, the other playing above them."

Dan: "It works a lot like the whammy bar on the guitar; you don't have to pump it madly to get more points, but you do have to do it at a constant pace. Play slowly or play fast but as long as the lanes are lit up, you're getting bonus points."

## BAND STRATEGY AND DYNAMICS

Grace: "Overdrive affects the entire Crowd Meter and everyone on it. For example, if your guitarist is in trouble, in a terrible solo, not doing well at all, and they don't have any overdrive—if band members take turns releasing overdrive, they can keep the guitarist going all the way through the solo."

Keith: "Play at your skill level when playing with a band. Don't step up and think you can do it, especially when the others can. You could be the reason the band fails."

### NOTE

A player can only be resurrected three times. If they fail a fourth time, the Crowd Meter starts to drop. When it reaches the bottom, the band fails the gig.

Dan: "The number one 'do' whenever you're playing is shed any embarrassment that you've got—belt out with your singing, don't be afraid to get on your knees and finger-tap the solos if you're playing guitar and go crazy on drums. Basically get into the spirit of playing in a band."

## THE MARATHON GIG

Before the team left us, they "accidentally" let this gem slip. Apparently there is a 58 song set. That's all 58 songs, played back-to-back-to-back-to…. You can pause it, but if you quit, or if a band member leaves, you fail and must restart the set from the beginning. However, get through it and you will be rewarded.

Now here's the crazy part: The reward is based on the lowest difficulty level that a band member selected. For example, if the entire band chooses Expert, you get the best reward. However, if one chooses Hard, you get the reward for completing it on Hard.

Keith, who's played it through three times says: "Play within your means, or one difficulty level less. Because there is nothing worse than being 47 songs into it and having a guy who chokes and can't play the rest of the way through!"

# ROCKBAND™

# TRAINING

If you want to improve your skills with any instrument or prepare for an upcoming gig, this is where you need to be. From the Training menu, you can choose, "Tutorials" or "Practice Mode." We strongly urge you to play through the tutorials for each instrument, before anything else.

After you finish the tutorials, check out Practice mode. This is a great tool that allows you to try out either entire songs or small pieces of songs, in order to improve your skills. Best of all, there is no Crowd Meter, so you needn't worry about failure.

If playing guitar, bass, or drums, you can choose the section of the song that you want to practice. If you want to play the entire song, simply select "Full Song." However, the purpose of practicing is to play the parts of the song you are struggling with. You can choose one or more parts to practice, and those sections will continue looping until you decide to exit.

**See the Set List for our recommendations on which pieces of each song you should practice.**

Finally, you are asked to select the speed at which your selection moves. If it's a particularly rapid section, start at 50% and gradually increase the speed as you get the hang of it. You can also change the speed while practicing using the control pad, so you're not locked into the choice you make here.

**Screen Shot 1.5: The practice screen**

Screen shot 1.5 shows the practice screen. Most of the elements that you find in the solo and multiplayer modes are disabled. There is no Crowd Meter, Energy meter, or score. You do receive a percentage rating though so you can judge how well you fared.

Now that you are familiar with Training mode, use it often and you'll see your skills increase dramatically.

# INSTRUMENTS

This chapter will cover the basics of using each instrument. Each section starts with a feature breakdown and then proceeds into a tutorial on how to use the instrument in conjunction with the game. Finally, we'll suggest songs that will help you learn basic, intermediate, and advanced techniques. This is a must-read chapter for beginners and seasoned players alike.

# DRUMS

Playing the drums is probably a brand-new experience for many of you. What follows is a step-by-step tutorial on setting up the kit and playing your first basic beat. You'll be up and drumming in no time!

## THE RACK

The drum kit consists of five pieces, as shown in diagram 2.1: On the rack are the red snare drum, the yellow high hat, the blue tom, and the green cymbal. On the floor is the orange kick drum. You play the pads with drumsticks and use your foot to strike the kick drum.

Diagram 2.1

Diagram 2.2

There is a standard way to hold the drumsticks in order to properly strike each pad (see Diagram 2.2). Grab the drumstick with your thumb and forefinger five to seven inches from the stick's bottom. The stick should rest in the space between your first and second knuckle. With a loose wrist, practice striking the pad, allowing the stick's head to bounce back after it makes contact. The stick's base should strike your palm at the same time the stick head strikes the drum pad.

Because the configuration of the drum kits used in each song may differ, from here on we only refer to the colors that mark each drum pad, rather than the piece itself.

13

The phrase "it's all in the wrist" is fitting for drummers who wish to build speed. Keep your forearm steady when you're playing, and let your wrist do all the work. This might be tough at first, and you can get through some of the more basic songs without heeding this advice, but if you want to become a skilled drummer, a loose grip and a flexible wrist are key ingredients to success.

Once you have the basic technique down, practice striking the red pad, alternating between your right and left hand and aiming for the pad's center. Start slow and gradually speed up to a decent tempo. When you're comfortable, try this exercise: Strike the red pad with your left stick, and then with your right. Strike the red pad again with your left hand, and then strike the yellow pad with your right. Follow it up by striking the red pad with left, and the blue pad with right. Get the idea? Move back and forth over the rack, speeding up as you go, until you consistently hit the center of each pad.

## THE KICK DRUM AND PROPER POSTURE/POSITION

Now let's move on to the kick drum. Place the pedal beneath the drum rack, fitting the grooves on its underside over the kit's base. This stabilizes the pedal. Now pull up a chair and have a seat. If the chair (or preferably a stool) you are using is adjustable, adjust it so that the tops of your thighs are parallel to the floor.

Place your foot on the pedal. Pull the chair forward until your ankle is directly beneath your knee. This will allow you to generate the most power and speed, as well as maximize your endurance.

When you are in the proper position, adjust the kit's height so that the bottom of the red pad is even with your forearm while playing. Notice that the pads are angled toward you. As your stick strikes the pad, match the stick's angle with the pads' angle. If you aren't driving the stick's tip directly into the pad, you'll get more bounce from your stick and will be able to play faster.

Now that you're in the proper position, rest your foot on the kick pedal, placing your heel on the pedal's flat surface. Depress the pedal a couple times, bringing your foot back up to its resting position each time. You can play with your heels up or down. Some drummers find they generate the most speed with their heel up, using their thigh to drive the pedal down. On the other hand, some drummers play with their heel on the floor, driving the pedal down with their calf. Try it both ways and see which is more comfortable.

If you are striking the rim a lot, either lower the drum kit or sit up straighter.

# THE DRUM TRACK

Now let's look at the onscreen prompts that will dictate what you'll play and when. Screen Shot 2.1 shows the drum track.

1. Notes (red, yellow, blue, or green)
2. Kick drum note (orange)
3. Target
4. Crowd Meter
5. Score
6. Energy meter
7. Multiplier meter

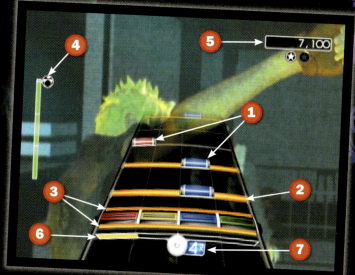

Screen Shot 2.1

Notes ( 1 ) come in four colors that match the colored rings on your drum pads. As each note crosses the target ( 3 ), strike the corresponding drum pad. A properly timed hit destroys the note, but a miss allows the note to escape, intact, beneath the target. The more notes you hit, the higher your score ( 5 ). Also, successfully striking consecutive notes moves the Drum icon on the Crowd Meter ( 4 ) higher and higher. Likewise, missing notes causes the Crowd Meter to fall. If the Crowd Meter hits bottom, you fail and must wait for a band member to revive you.

The kick drum note ( 2 ) looks different than the other notes—it is a thick orange line that cuts across the entire drum track. When it crosses the target, push down on the pedal to strike the note. If the kick drum note is beneath another note, then you must press the kick drum and strike the correct pad simultaneously.

The drum track contains a yellow horizontal line beneath the target. This is the Energy meter ( 6 ). The Energy meter fills up more and more as you successfully play specific strings of notes. When it hits or exceeds 50 percent, you can activate overdrive by striking the green note after a fill (see screen shots 2.2A and 2.2B).

Screen Shot 2.2A

Activate overdrive by striking the final green note after a fill. Screen shot 2.2B shows the drum track during overdrive.

Overdrive has two purposes. First, it riles up the crowd. This means they respond much more positively to you, or any band member, hitting a note. And, more importantly, they are less critical if you or any band member misses a note. Therefore, you should activate overdrive if you notice band mates faltering. Secondly, you can use overdrive to revive a fallen band member. It's automatic, so simply activate overdrive, and the fallen band member can resume playing.

The multiplier meter ( 7 ) increases the score gained by successfully playing notes. The higher the multiplier, the higher your score. Miss a note and the multiplier resets.

Learn more about the multiplier in the Touring and Training chapter.

## HAND- AND FOOTWORK

In *Rock Band*, there are two basic beats that require coordination of your hands and feet. They may be sped up or slowed down, but once you get the rhythm, it's all a matter of practice.

Check out screen shot 2.3. Notice that this beat requires continually striking the yellow pad, while intermittently striking the red pad and the orange kick drum. It may seem erratic, but there is a pattern. Here's how you learn it. Slowly at first, count from 1 to 4 repeatedly in your head. On every beat (1, 2, 3, and 4), strike the yellow pad with your right drumstick. Now, every time you reach 1, press the kick drum pedal. Finally, at every 3, strike the red pad with your left hand. Do this until you are comfortable and then gradually speed up the count in your head. You may even find that playing faster beats are easier!

Screen shot 2.4 shows a similar pattern, but here the blue pad replaces the yellow one. However, it's the same idea—keep constant time with your right stick, and strike the red pad and the kick at the correct intervals. You'll see many variations on these patterns as you play, but if you take the time to break them down, you'll be able to pick up the rhythm.

**Screen Shot 2.3**

**Screen Shot 2.4**

Congratulations, you are now familiar with the basics of drumming. It gets harder as the drum lines become more complex, but with a solid foundation and lots of practice, you'll be playing harder songs with ease.

If you find a song particularly difficult, select "Training" from the Main menu so you can practice it without fear of failure. You can also slow down the tempo of any song.

Some drummers keep the beat with their head, moving it back and forth in time. Others bounce in their chair. How you do it is up to you, but for now we suggest counting either out loud or in your head.

## PRACTICE

Lost and wondering what to play to get started? Here are some ideas to get you headed in the right direction. For basic beats, try The Strokes' "Reptilia" or Kiss's "Detroit Rock City" on Medium difficulty. For solid intermediate drum lines, practice Faith No More's "Epic" and the Smashing Pumpkins' "Cherub Rock" on Medium.

For the kick drum averse, try The Konk's "29 Fingers" and Timmy and the Lords of the Underworld's song of the same title.

After a rousing performance, it's okay to throw your drumsticks into the crowd; just make sure they're paying attention!

17

# ROCKBAND™

# GUITAR/BASS

Yes, we are grouping guitar and bass together. And, yes, we realize just how upset actual musicians are going to be. But grant us this one fault and we promise we won't commit any more grievous errors. For example, we won't call the bass a guitar or say that bassists who use picks are simply wannabe guitarists. Big of us, we know.

The reason we are combining the two sections is simple: The peripherals are the same. The Fender Stratocaster is used for playing both the guitar and the bass lines.

## THE GUITAR/BASS PERIPHERAL

Diagram 2.3

The guitar and bass peripheral has several components. Check out Diagram 2.3 and refer to the following list to understand them all:

**1** Frets
**2** High frets
**3** Strum bar
**4** Whammy bar
**5** Controls

The color-coded buttons on either end of the neck are the frets ( **1** ). The frets closest to the guitar's body are the high frets ( **2** ). They are named so because the closer you play to the guitar's body, the higher the notes. Therefore, playing the green fret produces a lower note than playing the orange fret.

The strum bar ( **3** ) acts as the strings on the guitar and bass. You strike up or down on it while pressing the fret to play a note.

The whammy bar ( **4** ) changes the pitch of a sustained note. While playing a sustained note, push the whammy bar toward the guitar's body to alter the note. The Five-Way-Switch (not pictured) affects the tone of your guitar or bass when overdrive is activated or during a guitar solo.

Finally, the controls ( **5** ) include a standard directional pad, along with a Start and Back button. Further, the frets act as control buttons—green for "accept" and red for "back."

# THE GUITAR/BASS TRACK

**Screen Shot 2.5**

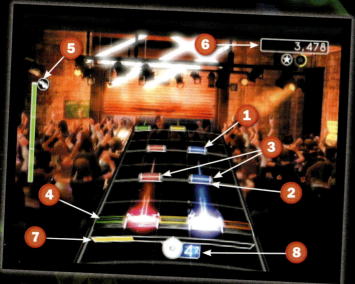

Screen shot 2.5 illustrates the onscreen guitar and bass track. Here is a breakdown of the components:

1. Notes (red, yellow, blue, green, or orange)
2. Sustained note
3. Chord
4. Target
5. Crowd Meter
6. Score
7. Energy meter
8. Multiplier meter

There are five different note colors: red, green, yellow, blue, and orange ( **1** ). Each corresponds to the colored frets on your guitar and bass. When a note crosses the target ( **4** ), you must simultaneously press the correct fret and strike the strum bar. Time it correctly and the note is played and destroyed. Miss it and the note escapes, usually making a twanging sound. Pressing the fret alone does nothing; you must also strum to play the note. Therefore, you are not penalized for holding down a fret in between notes.

Sustained notes ( **2** ) are notes that are held for a period of time. To play a sustained note, hold the correct fret and strum once, then release the strum bar and continue holding the fret down until the note ends.

Chords ( **3** ) are simply two or three notes played in unison. They can be adjacent notes like red/green, or separated notes like red/blue. To successfully play the chord, you must strum while holding down all the required frets.

The Crowd Meter ( **5** ) measures your accuracy while playing. Every note played correctly raises your meter, while every missed note lowers it. If your meter falls to zero, you fail the song. The Bass icon denotes the bassist's position on the meter, while the Guitar icon denotes the guitarist's position. Aside from raising the Crowd Meter, successfully playing notes raises your score ( **6** ).

The Energy meter ( **7** ) displays the amount of energy you have. You gain energy by flawlessly executing strings of specific notes. When the meter

During a guitar solo, you can simply press the high frets (no strumming required) to play the notes. If you choose to use the high frets during other parts of the song, you must also strum.

You need hold down only the fret when playing a sustained note, not the strum bar.

19

reads 50 percent or more, tilt the guitar to engage overdrive (see screen shot 2.4). Overdrive invigorates the crowd and makes them less critical of mistakes, helping you and your bandmates increase your respective Crowd Meters. It will also bring back a fallen band member, so use it wisely.

**Screen Shot 2.6**

The guitar/bass track during overdrive.

Finally, the Multiplier meter ( **8** ) rewards you for your accuracy. Every 10 notes you play successfully increases the multiplier. The higher your multiplier, the more points you earn per played note. However, miss a note and the multiplier resets.

## STANCES

Drummers have it easy; they get to lounge behind the drum kit all gig long and not worry about how they look. Guitarists and bassists, on the other hand, are on display, front and center. How they stand can positively or negatively affect a crowd's reaction to a specific solo or bass line, or to the show in general! With that kind of pressure, we thought it best to intervene.

So here, presented for your enjoyment and for the betterment of your musical career, are six stances to get you movin' on the road to stardom.

### STANDARD STANCE

Diagram 2.4 represents the Standard stance. This says to the crowd, "I'm really too cool to move much" and is generally used during songs with slower tempos. If you must use it, at least bob your head up and down to show the crowd you really do care (even if it's the 632nd time you've played the song in as many nights).

Diagram 2.4: Standard stance

## HEAVY STANCE

Notice the bent knees and the left foot out in front? This provides a stable base to absorb the shock of the heavy, crunchy, jackhammer-like guitar riffs you're laying down. It also allows you to whip your head around and wreck your neck to the furiously fast (or crushingly slow) beat.

**Diagram 2.5: Heavy stance**

## HIGH STANCE

Killing a particularly rabid solo? Then this is the stance to assume. The guitarist is so wicked that he doesn't even need to look at the frets!
This stance is also a good setup for a downward axe hack. After a bridge or break, when the guitar and drums are about to come roaring back, violently pull the neck of your guitar or bass toward the stage. Time it right, though, or you'll be slightly more ridiculed than a metal band doing a punk cover.

21

## LOW STANCE

This is sooo metal that you need to have quads of steel to pull it off. And look at that vertical neck; it says "hardcore" in more ways than one—the groupies will love it! And be sure to whip that hair back and forth while you're diggin' in to a frenetic solo or while playing so fast the strings are smokin'.

Diagram 2.7: Low stance

## POWER SLIDE

Did he just?? No way, that was friggin' rad!

Diagram 2.8:
Power Slide

## THROWIN' HORNS

A staple of metal since Ronnie James Dio first threw 'em up at a Sabbath concert over 25 years ago. People may argue its true meaning (if it even has one), but no one argues with its sheer power! And check it out, the kid is playing a solo on the high frets while raisin' his hands in a metal salute to the crowd. That's just downright sick!

**Diagram 2.9: Throwin' horns**

Showmanship should never interfere with your playing. Wait a minute…this is the entertainment industry. What are we saying? Go get 'em Milli Vanilli!

So there you have 'em, six stances to start a riot in the general admission section of your local arena. Use them all, but use them wisely, for the life you save could very well be your own.

## PRACTICE

There is a lot to learn if you're picking this up for the first time, but that's why we're here. We've identified a few common problem areas that beginner and intermediate players have in common and have compiled a list of song suggestions to help you out. It's a long road, but remember, the longest journey begins with the first fret!

## ALTERNATING NOTES

- The Who—"Won't Get Fooled Again": On bass, select Medium difficulty and practice Jam through Jam A.
- Beastie Boys—"Sabotage": On guitar, select Hard difficulty and practice the Intro through Verse 1. The higher, blue notes are constant but the lower, red notes are intermittent. You can keep both the red and the blue fret pressed constantly and still nail every note.

Only the highest fret you press counts when you strum. For example, if you see a long stream of alternating green and red notes, you can keep the green fret pressed even when you are playing the red notes.

23

## CHORD TRANSITIONS

Chord transitions simply refer to the movement of the fingers and hands when playing chords. An easy chord transition is green/red to red/yellow, while a more difficult one is green/yellow to red/blue. In the former case, you need not move your hand, but in the latter example, shifting your hand down the fret board is recommended.

- **Red Hot Chili Peppers—"Dani California":** On guitar, select Hard difficulty and practice the chorus.
- **Pixies—"Wave of Mutilation":** On guitar, select Hard difficulty and practice the intro.
- **Hole—"Celebrity Skin":** On guitar, select Hard difficulty.

The recessed fret buttons make it easy to slide your hand from one fret to the next as you would on an actual guitar or bass—but without the calluses!

## STEP-PROGRESSIONS

We define "step-progressions" as adjacent notes played one after the other. For example: green, red, yellow, and blue. At lower difficulty levels, the progressions are slow, but as the difficulty increases, so does the speed.

- **The Strokes—"Reptilia":** On guitar and bass, select Hard difficulty and practice the chorus.
- **The New Pornographers—"Electric Version":** On bass, select Hard difficulty.
- **The Who—"Won't Get Fooled Again":** On guitar, select Hard difficulty.
- **Coheed and Cambria—"Welcome Home":** On guitar, select Medium

difficulty and practice Verse 1. Also on guitar, select Hard difficulty to practice more advanced steps.

- **Tribe—"Outside":** On guitar, select Hard difficulty.

## CONSECUTIVE NOTES

Consecutive notes are simply notes of the same color that you play one after another. When they come fast and in large numbers, it's easy to let a few slip by the target, resetting your multiplier. Practice hitting them consistently.

- **The Police—"Next to You":** On bass, select Hard difficulty.
- **Deep Purple—"Highway Star":** On guitar, select Medium difficulty.
- **The Killers—"When You Were Young":** On guitar or bass, practice on Medium and Hard difficulties.
- **The Strokes—"Reptilia":** On bass, practice on Medium and Hard difficulties.
- **Vagiant—"Seven":** On bass, select Hard difficulty.

When facing long, rapid streams of consecutive notes, you'll need to strum both up and down on the strum bar.

## HAMMER-ONS AND PULL-OFFS

Hammer-ons are notes that are shorter than regular notes and can be played without strumming. Simply press the correct fret when the short notes cross the target. The catch is, you must hit the regular note that directly precedes the smaller-size note. To become an expert player, you absolutely must be able to pull these off.

A pull-off is the opposite of a hammer-on. Instead of striking a fret to play a note, you pull off one fret to play another note.

- Stone Temple Pilots—"Vaseline": On guitar, select Medium difficulty.
- Faith No More—"Epic": On bass, select Hard difficulty. Guitar Solo D has a 19-note hammer-on series.
- Beastie Boys—"Sabotage": On bass, select Hard difficulty.

# VOCALS

Know any good singers? We don't either, but we're gonna tell you how to score high using the microphone anyway.

## THE MICROPHONE

A microphone and a chord. That's it. Simple but definitely not easy. Oh, you sing or speak into the fat end.

Diagram 2.10

If you said "Oh" after we told you what side of the mic to sing into, hand the vocal duties over to someone else.

Screen shot 2.7: The vocal track

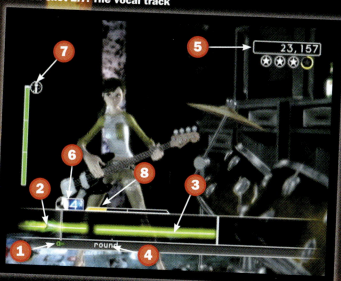

## THE VOCAL TRACK
1. Target
2. Pitch indicator
3. Notes
4. Lyrics
5. Score
6. Multiplier meter
7. Crowd Meter
8. Energy meter

Screen shot 2.7 shows the vocal track. The target ( 1 ) tells you when to start and stop singing. When the green note bar ( 3 ) crosses the target, start singing. When the tail end of the green note bar crosses the target, stop singing. That's the easy part.

## ROCK STAR

Ever find out the lyrics you thought you knew were nothing like the *actual* lyrics? For instance, it turns out that in "Cherub Rock", the words aren't "who wants heiney" but, "Who wants honey." The trick is to sing through your surprise and own the song.

The pitch indicator arrow (**2**) shows you what pitch (the level of sound) you are currently singing at. Your singing level must match the level of the oncoming notes (**3**). The lyrics (**4**) are provided so you know what to sing.

Sing consecutive phrases well and your Multiplier (**6**) increases. The higher the multiplier, the higher the points you receive (**5**).

Sometimes the song requires talking rather than singing. When necessary, the words will appear in the Lyric box (**4**) without any corresponding notes. Pitch doesn't matter here, so simply speak the words on time and you'll do fine.

Percussion notes (**3**) occasionally occur to give you something to do when you're not singing. Tap the head of the microphone against your hand when the note crosses the target.

**Screen shot 2.8A**

You are not penalized for missing or ignoring percussion notes. This is to allow singers the opportunity to also play an instrument.

The Energy meter (**8**) measures the amount of energy you have. You gain energy by nailing specific glowing phrases. When your Energy meter is at or above 50 percent, you can go into overdrive.

Activate overdrive by improvising during a freestyle section. Simply say "Go" or "Uh-huh" or something similar to activate overdrive. Check out screen shots 2.8A and 2.8B to see the vocal track in Overdrive mode.

**Screen shot 2.8B**

Screen shot 2.8A shows a freestyle section. Screen shot 2.8B shows the vocal track in Overdrive mode.

# SET LIST

Of the countless number of songs that exist, the folks at Harmonix have achieved the near-impossible task of choosing 58 to include in *Rock Band*. The selection process must have been daunting, but they managed to create a wonderful mix of genres that is sure to appeal to all players. It's guaranteed that you'll find songs you know and love. It's also just as likely that you'll come across songs you've never heard before. And that's where Prima comes in.

In the following pages, we'll break down every song by instrument and difficulty level (Medium and Hard), so you'll be prepared when asked to perform it as part of a band. We'll also illuminate the sections of the each song that you need to rehearse in order to increase your overall skill with your chosen instrument. Be it chord transitions, step-progressions, drum fills, holding notes, or whatever, we'll point out the most efficient way to learn them.

You'll definitely hear some new songs that you'll want to know more about. That's why we've included artist and album information for each song.

We also realize that the overall goal is to play as part of a band, be it for fun or in competition, with friends or online (online play is only available on the Xbox 360 and PS3 versions). To that end, we've included band-building strategy on each song. Have a new player and want to know what instrument to hand them? Want to score more points by playing on a higher difficulty but are afraid you might fail? If so, check out the "Band-Aid" section at the end of every song spread.

We've also included a table for each song that compares the relative difficulty of the bass, guitar, and drum lines (one star being the easiest; three stars being the hardest). Use the tables if, for example, you are searching for a bass line that trumps the guitar line. And we haven't ignored the singers—the star rankings included in the tables represent overall difficulty when compared to all the other songs. From half a star to five stars, you can tell at a glance what you're in for.

Before moving on, a quick explanation of our notation is in order. First, if we capitalize a portion of the song (i.e., "Chorus 1A"), that means it corresponds to a specific part of the song. You can select that portion while in Practice mode. If the portion of the song is *not* capitalized (i.e., "chorus"), then any chorus in the song will do.

Sometimes we list certain notes, like green or yellow. If the notes are separated by a forward slash (/), it represents a chord. So, "Press yellow/red" means press yellow *and* red at the same time, while "yellow to red" means the red note follows the yellow note.

Finally, some songs have "Big Rock Endings," which are fun to play and allow you to score BIG points, provided you pull them off! We've included a stamp to let you know if the song has a Big Rock Ending.

Well, that's all you need to know to make the best use of our guide, so go get 'em, rock star, and we'll see you on stage!

# "29 FINGERS"—THE KONKS

## BACKGROUND

**Album:** The Konks

**Released:** March 22, 2005

**Song Length:** 2:51

**Vocals:** Kurt

**Guitar:** Bob

**Bass:** Jon

**Drums:** Kurt

| DEVELOPER'S TOP SCORES ||
|------------|-----------|
| Bass | 59,941 |
| Drums | 92,575 |
| Guitar | 189,811 |
| Vocals | 8,462,818 |
| Band | 548,421 |

As both the drummer and the singer for The Konks, Kurt Davis props up his kit at the front of the stage using old record crates.

Kurt Davis protects his drum heads by covering them in duct tape. This also makes them sound pretty cool.

Collectively, The Konks have 29 fingers. Six of them are thumbs.

## REHEARSAL

| Difficulty Ranking |||||
|------------|-------|------|--------|--------|
| Difficulty | Drums | Bass | Guitar | Vocals |
| Medium | ★ | ★★ | ★★★ | ★★ |
| Hard | ★ | ★★ | ★★★ | |

## GUITAR

**Solo:** Yes
**Medium:** The Intro Riff will be tough for almost any intermediate guitarist. Best get the hang of it before playing with a band.
**Hard:** This is a tough song; to avoid certain failure, practice Verse 2B through Chorus 1 and the guitar solo.

## DRUMS

**Medium:** As the song says, "…only two lousy drums…." The entire song utilizes only the red snare and the blue tom.
**Hard:** If you can nail this song on Medium, you should have no trouble tackling it on Hard.

If you can't grasp the kick drum, this is the song for you!

## VOCALS

**Percussion:** Clap
**Notes:** Once you get the melody down, this song should be a smooth ride.

## BASS

**Medium:** Pretty straightforward, even for a new player.
**Hard:** A fun and difficult bass line. Play the Intro Riff through Verse B to master the pinky slide (shifting from the blue fret to the orange fret with your pinky).

# BAND AID

The bass line is straightforward, which is fortunate because the guitar lines aren't. Give guitar duty to a polished player and be ready to bring him back if he fails. And due to The Konks' two-piece drum kit, you can feel comfortable handing the sticks to a new player.

# "ARE YOU GONNA BE MY GIRL"—JET

## BACKGROUND

**Album:** Get Born

**Released:** September 14, 2003

**Song Length:** 3:34

**Vocals:** Nic Cester

**Guitar:** Nic Cester, Cameron Muncey

**Bass:** Mark Wilson

**Drums:** Chris Cester

| DEVELOPER'S TOP SCORES ||
| --- | --- |
| Bass | 21,921 |
| Drums | 135,775 |
| Guitar | 2,796,652 |
| Vocals | 8,167,996 |
| Band | 1,440,335 |

Jet named their band after a song by Paul McCartney's band Wings.

Reportedly, Jet founders Cameron Muncey and Nic Cester became best friends in their youth when they discovered they each had "Led Zeppelin" written on their bookbags.

## REHEARSAL

| Difficulty Ranking |||||
| --- | --- | --- | --- | --- |
| Difficulty | Drums | Bass | Guitar | Vocals |
| Medium | ★★★ | ★ | ★★ | ★★★♪ |
| Hard | ★★★ | ★ | ★★ | |

## GUITAR

**Solo:** Yes
**Medium:** Mostly green/red chords, but play through Chorus 1B to practice transitioning from green/red to red/yellow to yellow/blue and back to green/red.
**Hard:** Chorus 1 and Chorus 2 will test your ability to accurately and quickly shift your index and ring fingers up and down the entire fret board.

## DRUMS

**Medium:** If you've got a handle on basic beats, try the Guitar Solo for something a little different.
**Hard:** Rehearse Chorus 2A and the Guitar Solo.

## VOCALS

**Percussion:** Yes
**Notes:** The talking parts that are spaced throughout the song can be real lifesavers, so don't blow 'em.

## BASS

**Medium:** Good practice for making red to yellow and yellow to red transitions.
**Hard:** Select Chorus 3 and practice crushing the higher notes.

## BAND AID

You can get away with an inexperienced bass player, but make sure you have a seasoned drummer. An intermediate guitarist can handle the licks on Hard. Keep an eye on your singer to see if he or she needs a boost.

31

# "BALLROOM BLITZ"—
## AS MADE FAMOUS BY SWEET *

### DETAILS ON THE CLASSIC

**Album:** Desolation Boulevard

**Released:** August 1973

**Song Length:** 4:06

**Vocals:** Brian Connolly

**Guitar:** Andy Scott

**Bass:** Steve Priest

**Drums:** Mick Tucker

| DEVELOPER'S TOP SCORES | |
|---|---|
| Bass | 146,157 |
| Drums | 138,520 |
| Guitar | 228,999 |
| Vocals | 6,385,105 |
| Band | 3,058,251 |

Sweet's Mick Tucker and Deep Purple's Ian Gillan were originally in a band called "Wainwright's Gentlemen."

"Ballroom Blitz" was reportedly conceived when the members of Sweet were forced to leave the stage due to "a shower of bottles" during a concert in Scotland.

## REHEARSAL

| Difficulty Ranking | | | | |
|---|---|---|---|---|
| Difficulty | Drums | Bass | Guitar | Vocals |
| Medium | ★★★ | ★ | ★★ | |
| Hard | ★★★ | ★ | ★★ | ★★♪ |

* This is a cover version of a song made famous by the artist indicated.

## GUITAR

**Solo:** Yes
**Medium:** Although short, Outro A might cause you to falter the first couple times you play it.
**Hard:** You best be very good before attempting this one. Practice Chorus 3B through Guitar Solo 3 until you nail it.

## DRUMS

**Medium:** Practice Drum Intro through Band Enters, as the pattern is repeated throughout the song.
**Hard:** Rehearse Outro A through Guitar Solo C to ensure you don't fail when it comes to playing a gig.

## VOCALS

**Percussion:** Clap
**Notes:** The lengthy talking parts are enough to save a singer who's struggling to keep up with the lyrics' fast pace and high pitch.

## BASS

**Medium:** Select Chorus 1A and 1B and get used to the consecutive notes that require a quick double tap on the strum bar.
**Hard:** Practice Verse 1 until you get the hang of hitting every blue note. Not perfecting these sections is a surefire way to ruin your score multiplier when on tour.

## BAND AID

Only very experienced players should attempt this song on higher difficulties. The bass line is bearable, but every other instrument is unforgiving. If they can keep up with the talking parts, singers can select a higher difficulty than they are used to.

33

# "BLACK HOLE SUN"— SOUNDGARDEN

## BACKGROUND

**Album:** Superunknown

**Released:** March 8, 1994

**Song Length:** 5:17

**Vocals:** Chris Cornell

**Guitar:** Kim Thyil, Chris Cornell

**Bass:** Ben Shepherd

**Drums:** Matt Cameron

| DEVELOPER'S TOP SCORES | |
|---|---|
| Bass | 49,412 |
| Drums | 179,080 |
| Guitar | 2,328,679 |
| Vocals | 23,225,300 |
| Band | 4,707,020 |

Soundgarden named themselves after a sculpture on public display in their native Seattle.

Soundgarden singer Chris Cornell was originally also the band's drummer.

## REHEARSAL

| Difficulty Ranking | | | | |
|---|---|---|---|---|
| Difficulty | Drums | Bass | Guitar | Vocals |
| Medium | ★★★ | ★ | ★★ | ★♪ |
| Hard | ★★★ | ★ | ★★ | |

## GUITAR

**Solo:** Yes
**Medium:** Practice Chorus 2 if you have trouble transitioning from green/red to yellow/blue to red/yellow.
**Hard:** Practice Verse 2 and Guitar Solo A and B if you need help shifting your hand down the fret board (start with your index finger on red).

## DRUMS

**Medium:** Play from Chorus 3 through the Outro; it may throw novice drummers, but the slow tempo makes it very forgiving.
**Hard:** The verses should pose no problem for experienced drummers. Instead, concentrate on the choruses, the guitar solo, and the outro.

## VOCALS

**Percussion:** No
**Notes:** You better be able to hold a note at a low pitch or the chorus will ruin you. Practice it before you take the stage with your band.

## BASS

**Medium:** The song's first half is a lesson on playing sustained notes.
**Hard:** More sustained notes, but with orange ones thrown in.

Remember, there is no need to hold the strum bar during a sustained note, just the fret.

## BAND AID

This song's slow tempo makes it great for beginner drummers to step up to Medium difficulty. However, it takes a good drummer to handle the song on Hard. Put your best string player on guitar, as the bass line is very simple. If your singer can hold a note, they should have no problem tackling this on Medium.

# "BLITZKRIEG BOP"— RAMONES

## DEVELOPER'S TOP SCORES

| | |
|---|---|
| Bass | 35,275 |
| Drums | 174,920 |
| Guitar | 2,805,661 |
| Vocals | 3,927,430 |
| Band | 8,427,971 |

## BACKGROUND

**Album:** Ramones

**Released:** November 1975

**Song Length:** 2:10

**Vocals:** Joey Ramone

**Guitar:** Johnny Ramone

**Bass:** Dee Dee Ramone

**Drums:** Tommy Ramone

Dee Dee Ramone quit the band in 1989. His post-Ramones activities included putting out a rap album, playing in a Ramones spin-off band called the Ramainz, and writing a really weird novel.

Tommy Ramone took the drum throne for the Ramones when no one else wanted the job. Up until then, he was happy managing the band.

The first Ramones album featured 14 songs and was less than 30 minutes in length.

## REHEARSAL

### Difficulty Ranking

| Difficulty | Drums | Bass | Guitar | Vocals |
|---|---|---|---|---|
| Medium | ★★★ | ★ | ★★ | ♪ |
| Hard | ★★★ | ★ | ★★ | |

## GUITAR

**Solo:** No

**Medium:** Fairly straightforward and repetitious. Those going for high consecutive note streaks should perfect this one.

**Hard:** Select Verse 1 if you're having trouble transitioning from green/yellow to yellow/orange.

## DRUMS

**Medium:** Remember to count if you're having trouble keeping up with the beat. This is a standard drum beat, which you must master before moving on to Hard.

**Hard:** Pretty standard fare for advanced drummers. The rest of us should perfect the intermediate beats before attempting.

## VOCALS

**Percussion:** No

**Notes:** A good song for a novice singer to practice. It's fast, but once you learn the cadence, you'll have no problem.

In order to score high, nail the rising and falling notes at the end of each phrase.

## BASS

**Medium:** A punk song played on Medium is like a heavy metal band doing a ballad—pointless.

**Hard:** As with a lot of these songs, the better you know it, the better you'll do. The slight pauses in between scores of notes are easy to play over, but a trained ear will pick up the rhythm and adjust accordingly.

# BAND AID

Hard may cause problems for unseasoned guitarists and drummers, but intermediate bassists can handle a higher difficult level. For a challenge, the bassist can also take on vocal duties.

# ROCKBAND™

# "BLOOD DOLL"— ANARCHY CLUB

## BACKGROUND

**Album:** A Single Drop of Red

**Released:** 11/07

**Length:** 3:35

**Vocals:** Keith Smith

**Guitar:** Keith Smith & Adam Buhler

**Bass:** Adam Buhler

**Drummer:** Robyn Graves (Special Guest)

| DEVELOPER'S TOP SCORES | |
|---|---|
| Bass | 33,611 |
| Drums | 101,975 |
| Guitar | 110,313 |
| Vocals | 10,499,446 |
| Band | 756,503 |

Anarchy Club's original name was Fearless Vampire Killers, inspired by a song from the legendary Bad Brains.

Keith Smith got his first guitar lesson in the hallway of a Rhode Island motel. Oh, and it was from Kurt Cobain.

Hey, lil' rockers, it's never too early to start covering your school notebooks with metal symbols such as the anarchy icon. Your teachers and parents will love it!

## REHEARSAL

| Difficulty Ranking | | | | |
|---|---|---|---|---|
| Difficulty | Drums | Bass | Guitar | Vocals |
| Medium | ★★★ | ★ | ★★ | |
| Hard | ★★★ | ★ | ★★ | ★★★♪ |

## GUITAR

**Solo:** Yes
**Medium:** Practice Verse 1 if you need help hitting the blue fret with your pinky finger.
**Hard:** Practice Verse 1 and learn to hit the blue and the orange frets from the home position (index finger on green). It's a nice pinky stretch.

## DRUMS

**Medium:** A good tempo and a steady beat make this a good song for intermediate drummers who need to work on basic rhythms.
**Hard:** If intermittent double-kick-drum notes don't bother you, then you'll be able to play through this song with little trouble.

## VOCALS

**Percussion:** No
**Notes:** Let out your most sinister laugh after the talking part; it'll engage overdrive, but more importantly it just sounds cool.

## BASS

**Medium:** If you can ace Verse 1 and Chorus 1, then it's time to try the song on a harder difficulty.
**Hard:** Practice the choruses until you can consistently hit the higher notes. Your index finger should be on the red fret when you play through it.

## BAND AID

A band with just a little experience will have a good time playing this song on Medium difficulty. An all-around solid band should feel comfortable selecting Hard for all instruments.

39

# "BRAINPOWER"—FREEZEPOP

## BACKGROUND

| DEVELOPER'S TOP SCORES | |
| --- | --- |
| Bass | 89,480 |
| Drums | 116,600 |
| Guitar | 89,327 |
| Vocals | 5,241,457 |
| Band | 464,029 |

**Album:** future future future perfect

**Released:** 2007

**Length:** 2:10

**Vocals:** Liz Enthusiasm

**Guitar:** Duke of Pannekoeken

**Bass:** Sean Drinkwater

**Drummer:** Duke/Sean

When people tour outside the United States, Freezepop says people should say they're from "near Canada."

Freezepop got arrested trying to enter Canada under false pretenses.

Don't get arrested in Canada like Freezepop.

## REHEARSAL

| Difficulty Ranking | | | | |
| --- | --- | --- | --- | --- |
| Difficulty | Drums | Bass | Guitar | Vocals |
| Medium | ★★★ | ★ | ★★ | ★★♪ |
| Hard | ★★★ | ★ | ★★ | |

## GUITAR

**Solo:** Yes
**Medium:** This song is tough for Medium, but Verse 1 gives you a good chance to practice your pull-offs.
**Hard:** If you aren't adept at executing hammer-ons at a rapid pace, this song will surely trip you up. Practice Verse 1 and try to pull off the long string of them.

## DRUMS

**Medium:** The quick tempo might be too much for beginner drummers, but it's still the same basic beat you've played in many of the other songs. Keep practicing and your hands and feet will catch up to your eyes.
**Hard:** Practice Chorus 1 and if you have trouble, ignore one of the double kick drums. Get your hands working in time with your foot, and *then* try to add the second kick drum.

## VOCALS

**Percussion:** No
**Notes:** It's Bananarama meets Thomas Dolby, but with a sense of humor! We can't get enough! Oh, and you're gonna laugh when you read the words—just don't let 'em throw you off track.

## BASS

**Medium:** Remember to keep your finger planted on the lower fret as you're playing the alternating streams of green and yellow notes. This reduces the fatigue caused by repetitive motion.
**Hard:** While practicing the intro, do your best to minimize strumming by hitting the hammer-ons. However, if you fall out of rhythm, get back into it by strumming through them like they were regular notes.

# BAND AID

A quick tempo and rapidly moving notes make this song tough to play on Medium, let alone Hard. If you question your capabilities, select Easy or Medium.

# "CAN'T LET GO"— DEATH OF THE COOL

## BACKGROUND

**Album:** N/A

**Released:** 2007

**Length:** 3:35

**Vocals:** Izzy Maxwell

**Guitar:** Izzy Maxwell

**Bass:** Izzy Maxwell

**Drummer:** Jeff Allen

**Synths:** Pete Maguire

| DEVELOPER'S TOP SCORES | |
|---|---|
| Bass | 82,402 |
| Drums | 112,225 |
| Guitar | 142,942 |
| Vocals | 7,703,587 |
| Band | 599,755 |

Death of the Cool's drummer Jeff Allen sometimes uses his mutton chops as fifth and sixth limbs to play the really tricky beats.

Izzy Maxwell, Jeff Allen, and Pete Maguire are half of the Harmonix audio department and all of Death of the Cool.

Death of the Cool is one of those pretentious bands that tries to look cool by pretending not to be.

Death of the Cool consists of the members of Count Zero, Breaking Wheel, and inter:sect.

## REHEARSAL

| Difficulty Ranking | | | | |
|---|---|---|---|---|
| Difficulty | Drums | Bass | Guitar | Vocals |
| Medium | ★★★ | ★ | ★★ | ★★★★★ |
| Hard | ★★★ | ★ | ★★ | |

## GUITAR

**Solo:** Yes
**Medium:** Select Bridge through Bridge A for some difficult chord transitions.
**Hard:** The Guitar Solo and Chorus 3 throw some fast step-progressions and lots of hammer-on notes at you. You might need to reduce the speed a bit to catch on.

## DRUMS

**Medium:** The Chorus provides a nice break to the monotonous kick/high hat/snare beat that by now we're all used to.
**Hard:** The Outro provides a challenge, even for skilled drummers. It's time to see if your hands are as quick as your feet.

## VOCALS

**Percussion:** No
**Notes:** If you are having trouble hitting the highs or lows on this track, remember, there is no penalty for singing during empty sections. Use the time to find the correct pitch.

The original lineup for Death of the Cool was a cat and a dog. The cat knew karate. The dog knew "sit" and "heel."

## BASS

**Medium:** Select the Outro to rehearse hitting the bundles of continuous notes.
**Hard:** Practice Chorus 3 until you can nail rapid red, yellow, and blue step-progressions.

If you are having trouble performing fast step-progressions, it helps to look at each note in turn as it's played (rather than always looking to the next set). It's like your old coach used to say, "Keep your eye on the ball!"

Death of the Cool might remind you of what the B-52s would sound like if they penned an album right after all their dogs died in a freak electrical storm.

## BAND AID

Hand your strongest members the drumsticks and the guitar. If they aren't highly experienced, Medium difficulty is the best choice.

# "CELEBRITY SKIN"—HOLE

## BACKGROUND

**Album:** Celebrity Skin

**Released:** September 8, 1998

**Song Length:** 2:42

**Vocals:** Courtney Love

**Guitar:** Eric Erlandson

**Bass:** Melissa Auf der Maur

**Drums:** Samantha Maloney (uncredited)

| DEVELOPER'S TOP SCORES | |
|---|---|
| Bass | 144,320 |
| Drums | 176,600 |
| Guitar | 2,419,066 |
| Vocals | 3,320,000 |
| Band | 3,603,081 |

Hole bassist Melissa Auf der Maur eventually replaced the Smashing Pumpkins' D'arcy Wretzky. Auf der Maur has since been replaced by Ginger Reyes, formerly of the Halo Friendlies.

Former Hole bassist Melissa Auf der Maur was also the frontwoman for Hand of Doom, a Black Sabbath cover band.

Courtney Love performed "Celebrity Skin" topless at the 1999 Big Day Out Festival in Australia.

## REHEARSAL

| Difficulty Ranking | | | | |
|---|---|---|---|---|
| Difficulty | Drums | Bass | Guitar | Vocals |
| Medium | ★★★ | ★ | ★★ | ★★ |
| Hard | ★★ | ★ | ★★★ | |

## GUITAR

**Solo:** No
**Medium:** Practice Bridge 1 through Bridge 1A, as it'll cause an intermediate guitarist trouble.
**Hard:** This whole song is a tutorial on advanced chord transitions. Also, practice the bridge because it's a beast—slow it down to 70 percent to get the feel for it.

## DRUMS

**Medium:** If the song is giving you trouble, start out practicing Bridge 1 through Bridge 1A and then move on to the chorus.
**Hard:** Rehearse Chorus 1 to learn the song's unique progressions.

## VOCALS

**Percussion:** No
**Notes:** The lows and highs might cause novice singers problems, but if you can nail the middle notes consistently, you should be fine.

Courtney Love appeared in the film *Sid and Nancy*, playing Nancy Spungen's best friend, Gretchen.

## BASS

**Medium:** Practice Verse 2 if you have problems hitting the blue notes.
**Hard:** Practicing Verse 2 through Chorus 2 will help you nail those high-note transitions.

Courtney Love was once the lead singer of Faith No More.

# BAND AID

If you have an apt drummer who can keep up with standard drum beats, then all you need to worry about is your guitar player, as some of the transitions are tough and require nimble finger-work.

45

# "CHERUB ROCK"—SMASHING PUMPKINS

## BACKGROUND

**Album:** Siamese Dream

**Released:** July 27, 1993

**Song Length:** 4:58

**Vocals:** Billy Corgan

**Guitar:** James Iha, Billy Corgan

**Bass:** D'Arcy Wretzky

**Drums:** Jimmy Chamberlin

| DEVELOPER'S TOP SCORES | |
|---|---|
| Bass | 152,514 |
| Drums | 237,031 |
| Guitar | 225,315 |
| Vocals | 13,411,531 |
| Band | 2,072,347 |

Billy Corgan, vocalist/guitarist for Smashing Pumpkins, released a book of poetry in 2004.

Ozzy Osbourne's wife, Sharon, was briefly the Smashing Pumpkins' manager.

## REHEARSAL

| Difficulty Ranking | | | | |
|---|---|---|---|---|
| Difficulty | Drums | Bass | Guitar | Vocals |
| Medium | ★★★ | ★ | ★★ | ★★✦ |
| Hard | ★★★ | ★ | ★★ | |

## GUITAR

**Solo:** No
**Medium:** Play through Chorus 1 to see if you have any trouble playing adjacent chords. Remember, in the transition from yellow/blue to red/yellow, the finger on yellow stays put.
**Hard:** This song throws every trick at you to test what you have learned. You must be able to constantly shift your hand position on the fret board, play hammer-ons and pull-offs, perform rapid chord transitions, and execute quick step-progressions. After Verse 1, it settles down a bit, so be sure to practice the Intro through Verse 1.

## DRUMS

**Medium:** This is a really fun song to play. It departs just enough from the basic patterns you've played many times before but remains very accessible to intermediate drummers. Practice the Intro through Main Riff 1 to learn the progression.
**Hard:** What makes an apt drummer is the ability to play different rhythms with each hand and foot. To reach the next level, run through this song and ignore the kick drum. When you get the rhythm, run through the song, playing only the kick drum. Finally, start putting both pieces together. It'll take some time, but the difficulty makes it a worthy challenge.

## VOCALS

**Percussion:** No
**Notes:** Don't oversing this song while trying to reach the high-pitched notes. You should be able to hone in on the correct pitch and get through the song.

Verse 1 on Hard is a nice, easy tutorial on hammer-ons. Even if you're a beginner, practice it until you get 'em all.

## BASS

**Medium:** The Intro Riff is repeated; make sure you are comfortable pulling off the broken stream of continuous notes so you don't blow your multiplier while onstage.
**Hard:** This song tests your command of the green and yellow frets. Practice Intro and Main Riff 1 to become familiar with the rapid hammer-ons and pull-offs.

# BAND AID

This song played on Medium should be challenging enough for most bands. Take it to the next level at your own risk, as the guitar and drums are very difficult. Hand the vocal duties over to someone with a high-pitched voice and they'll thrive.

# "CREEP"—RADIOHEAD

## BACKGROUND

**Album:** Pablo Honey

**Released:** February 22, 1993

**Song Length:** 3:56

**Vocals:** Thom Yorke

**Guitar:** Jonny Greenwood

**Bass:** Colin Greenwood

**Drums:** Phil Selway

| DEVELOPER'S TOP SCORES ||
| --- | --- |
| Bass | 87,872 |
| Drums | 163,000 |
| Guitar | 2,426,392 |
| Vocals | 12,968,110 |
| Band | 6,660,227 |

Radiohead's lead guitarist, Jonny Green-wood, originally joined the band as a harmonica player.

Radiohead's lineup has never changed since forming under the name "On a Friday" in 1986.

## REHEARSAL

| Difficulty Ranking | | | | |
| --- | --- | --- | --- | --- |
| Difficulty | Drums | Bass | Guitar | Vocals |
| Medium | ★★★ | ★ | ★★ | ★ |
| Hard | ★★★ | ★ | ★★ | |

# GUITAR

**Solo:** No
**Medium:** Pretty simple stuff, but the chorus is fun to practice.
**Hard:** The choruses are great for learning to shift your hand up and down the fret board, while the bridge teaches you to strum both up and down.

# DRUMS

**Medium:** Pretty standard beat all the way through, but practice the nifty transition within the bridge.
**Hard:** Practice the transition from Chorus 2 to the bridge.

# VOCALS

**Percussion:** No
**Notes:** You gotta belt out and sustain high notes during the bridge, but the rest of the song is pretty even-pitched.

# BASS

**Medium:** A perfect song for a novice to step up to Medium difficulty. Practice the bridge if you're having trouble.
**Hard:** Practice Chorus 2 if you need to work on your hammer-ons.

# BAND AID

This is a perfect song to gauge each band member's proficiency. The beats and riffs are pretty standard on each difficulty, so you'll quickly be able to tell who is playing above or below their potential. A singer who has a little range can hold their own.

# "DANI CALIFORNIA"— RED HOT CHILI PEPPERS

## BACKGROUND

**Album:** Stadium Arcadium

**Released:** May 5, 2006

**Song Length:** 4:42

**Vocals:** Anthony Kiedis

**Guitar:** John Frusciante

**Bass:** Flea

**Drums:** Chad Smith

| DEVELOPER'S TOP SCORES | |
|---|---|
| Bass | 273,225 |
| Drums | 232,175 |
| Guitar | 3,748,339 |
| Vocals | 17,851,484 |
| Band | 1,212,543 |

The first Red Hot Chili Peppers gig consisted of one song. Based on the enthusiastic audience response, they were invited to return for another set...of TWO songs.

Before settling on their current band name, the Red Hot Chili Peppers once considered calling themselves "Spigot Blister and the Chest Pimps."

## REHEARSAL

### Difficulty Ranking

| Difficulty | Drums | Bass | Guitar | Vocals |
|---|---|---|---|---|
| Medium | ★★★ | ★ | ★★ | ★★ |
| Hard | ★★ | ★ | ★★★ | |

## GUITAR

**Solo:** Yes

**Medium:** Select Chorus 1 to work on your chord transitions. If you're having trouble, try shifting your hand down the fret board.

**Hard:** There are some wicked sections in this song that may stump even the most experienced players. Practice Verse 1A and Outro Solo A through Outro Solo B for a course in advanced hammer-ons.

## DRUMS

**Medium:** Practice the verses for the snare/high-hat combo and the choruses for the cymbal/snare combo.

**Hard:** Practice Chorus 1 to get the hang of the alternating green and red notes.

## VOCALS

**Percussion:** Yes

**Notes:** Smooth, long notes during the chorus and quick, short notes through the verses make this a fun song to sing.

If you're a true Red Hot Chili Peppers fan, you'll perform wearing only a sock...and not on your foot.

## BASS

**Medium:** Not the hardest bass line to follow, but it moves fairly quickly, and there's very little downtime. Practice Verse 1A to 2B and you'll pick it up in no time.

**Hard:** This one gets pretty tough, but what'd you expect from a Flea composition? Select the bridge and Outro Solo A to practice your hammer-ons.

## BAND AID

Even experienced guitarists and bassists might be in over their heads the first few times they attempt this song on Hard. Unless they're very well-practiced, everyone should select Medium.

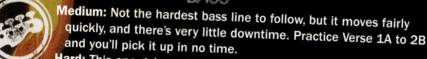

51

# "DAY LATE, DOLLAR SHORT"— THE ACROBRATS

## DEVELOPER'S TOP SCORES

| | |
|---|---|
| Bass | — |
| Drums | 136,325 |
| Guitar | 116,799 |
| Vocals | 7,587,559 |
| Band | 891,611 |

## BACKGROUND

**Album:** …Go Down Swinging

**Released:** 5/2006

**Length:** 3:02

**Vocals:** Chris

**Guitar:** Chris/Daniel

**Bass:** Swid

**Drummer:** Eliahu

Don't ask The Acrobrats' bassist, Swid Brat, to explain germanium transistors. Unless you're really, really, really into germanium transistors.

The Acrobrats' bassist, Swid Brat, builds complex amps and pedals from scratch, which is pretty impressive. What's more impressive is that he still hasn't fixed Daniel Brat's backup head that he broke two years ago.

## REHEARSAL

### Difficulty Ranking

| Difficulty | Drums | Bass | Guitar | Vocals |
|---|---|---|---|---|
| Medium | ★★★ | ★ | ★★ | ★★★★★ |
| Hard | ★★ | ★★ | ★ | |

## GUITAR

**Solo:** Yes
**Medium:** Select Verse 2 to practice green/yellow to red/blue chord transitions.
**Hard:** Practice Verse 1 and Verse 2 to perfect the rapid chord transitions. There's also a nice blue/orange to yellow/blue to red/yellow transition during the Guitar Solo you have try.

There is no need to lift your fingers when moving between green/yellow and red/blue.
Simply slide your hand back and forth.

## DRUMS

**Medium:** The fast tempo makes this a tough song for intermediate drummers. Practice Verse 3 and the Bridge until you can keep up.
**Hard:** There are lots of fills in this song, which makes staying on beat difficult. Practice the Bridge and see if you can nail every note.

## VOCALS

**Percussion:** Yes
**Notes:** A fun guitar riff and a catchy chorus help singers unfamiliar with this song keep on track. These phrases are packed with words, which will test your ability to pull off quick, clipped notes.

The multiplier resets when you miss a note *and* when you strum where there is no note.

## BASS

**Medium:** Practice Chorus 3 if you need to work on your step-progressions.
**Hard:** We've dubbed this song the "Multiplier Destroyer" because of its furious tempo and broken streams of continuous notes. Not only do you have to strum like a jackhammer, but you also have to strum accurately.

## BAND AID

You need a good drummer to get through this song on any difficulty. Furthermore, make sure your bassist selects Medium if you're relying on him or her to revive a weaker player, as the song's speed makes it easy to drop a few notes.

53

# "DEAD ON ARRIVAL"— FALLOUT BOY

## BACKGROUND

**Album:** Take This to Your Grave

**Released:** May 6, 2003

**Song Length:** 3:14

**Vocals:** Patrick Stump

**Guitar:** Joe Trohman

**Bass:** Pete Wentz

**Drums:** Andy Hurley

| DEVELOPER'S TOP SCORES | |
|---|---|
| Bass | 67,426 |
| Drums | 93,675 |
| Guitar | 186,074 |
| Vocals | 313,395 |
| Band | 1,094,634 |

The members of Fall Out Boy, along with a handful of other popular bands, opened a bar in NYC in order to have a respite from typical New York nightlife.

Fall Out Boy's guitarist, Joe Trohman, reportedly bought his first half-stack guitar amp with his bar mitzvah money.

## REHEARSAL

| Difficulty Ranking | | | | |
|---|---|---|---|---|
| Difficulty | Drums | Bass | Guitar | Vocals |
| Medium | ★★★ | ★ | ★★ | ★★★ |
| Hard | ★★★ | ★ | ★★ | |

## GUITAR

**Medium:** A quick tempo and a lot of notes make this a fun song for intermediate bassists. Practice Chorus 3 through the Outro and you'll be ready to hit the stage.

**Hard:** The saying goes, "The songs you grow to like, never stick at first." And you won't like this song unless you practice the Intro in addition to Verse 1A through Guitar Solo A.

## DRUMS

**Medium:** Play through Verse 2 a few times and you'll be good to take on this song with a band.

**Hard:** Inexperienced drummers and those prone to seizures should avoid this song. You gotta be able to play notes immediately before and after each kick to succeed.

## VOCALS

**Percussion:** Yes

**Notes:** A fun song with varied intonations. If you have a little range and the energy to keep up, you'll see this song through to the end.

## BASS

**Medium:** Don't get used to just mashing the strum bar. Select Verse 1 and notice the 3-1-3 pattern. This is repeated through the song, so learn it and don't screw it up on stage.

**Hard:** Your index finger should spend most of this song above the red fret. Shift back to the home position only when you need to grab the rare series of green notes.

There is no playing this song standing still. It's fast and frenetic, so respond in kind! Hop, jump, bounce, headbang and whip your guitar from side to side. On stage, showmanship counts.

A fast tempo makes this a relatively hard song, no matter the difficulty. Make sure you've warmed up or it'll catch you off guard.

# "DETROIT ROCK CITY"—KISS

## BACKGROUND

**Album:** Destroyer

**Released:** March 15, 1976

**Song Length:** 5:17

**Vocals:** Paul Stanley

**Guitar:** Ace Frehley

**Bass:** Gene Simmons

**Drums:** Peter Criss

| DEVELOPER'S TOP SCORES | |
|---|---|
| Bass | 70,451 |
| Drums | 158,725 |
| Guitar | 1,905,850 |
| Vocals | 7,248,880 |
| Band | 10,252,442 |

## BIG ROCK ENDING!

In the mid-seventies, two KISS comic books were released. Allegedly, the band members' blood was mixed with the red ink used to print the books.

KISS guitarist Ace Frehley was electrocuted at a concert in 1976 and, after treatment, returned to the stage to finish the show.

## REHEARSAL

| Difficulty Ranking | | | | |
|---|---|---|---|---|
| Difficulty | Drums | Bass | Guitar | Vocals |
| Medium | ★★★ | ★ | ★★ | ★★★ |
| Hard | ★★★ | ★ | ★★ | |

## GUITAR

**Solo:** Yes

**Medium:** Pretty clear-cut, so practice Bridge A through Bridge B to nail the solo.

**Hard:** You gotta nail the Guitar Riff and the solo (Bridge A and Bridge B) to call yourself worthy!

## DRUMS

**Medium:** It pays to keep a four count during this song: Play a constant high hat, the kick drum on 1, and the snare at 2 and 4.

**Hard:** Practice the verses to get the rapid-fire kick drum down.

A *real* guitarist would use the high frets during the solo! Consider yourself called out.

You get a break during the bridge; use it to amp up the crowd. Shouting, "Hey, Hey, Hey…" is always recommended.

## VOCALS

**Percussion:** Yes

**Notes:** The steep drops will throw singers who can't hit the higher notes. Fortunately, the chorus is pretty even in pitch, so you can make up for poor performance there.

## BASS

**Medium:** Play this any more than one time on Medium and you'll get a tongue-lashing from Gene!

**Hard:** Practice the transitions during the Guitar Riff until you perfect 'em.

## BAND AID

There are a couple of sections in each difficulty level that will challenge players of the respective experience level. Just do your best and power through those parts. Oh, and if you don't like failure, put a consistent drummer on the skins.

# "(DON'T FEAR) THE REAPER"— BLUE ÖYSTER CULT

| DEVELOPER'S TOP SCORES ||
|---|---|
| Bass | 143,680 |
| Drums | 350,860 |
| Guitar | 3,818,431 |
| Vocals | 9,712,594 |
| Band | 16,674,473 |

## BACKGROUND

**Album:** Agents of Fortune

**Released:** May 1976

**Song Length:** 5:09

**Vocals:** Eric Bloom

**Guitar:** Eric Bloom

**Bass:** Joe Bouchard, Allen Lanier

**Drums:** Albert Bouchard

Blue Öyster Cult singer Eric Bloom claims that he was the cowbell player on "Don't Fear the Reaper." Former bassist Joe Bouchard, however, says that the cowbell virtuoso was his brother Albert.

Blue Öyster Cult formed in 1967 under the name "Soft White Underbelly."

## REHEARSAL

| Difficulty Ranking |||||
|---|---|---|---|---|
| Difficulty | Drums | Bass | Guitar | Vocals |
| Medium | ★★ | ★ | ★★★ | ★ |
| Hard | ★★ | ★ | ★★★ | |

## GUITAR

**Solo:** Yes
**Medium:** Try playing through the break without lifting your finger off the red fret.
**Hard:** Practice the break; the rapid red-to-blue-to-orange transitions require fast fingers.

## DRUMS

**Medium:** Practice the entire guitar solo and the entire outro so you're not caught off guard when playing this with your band.
**Hard:** Select Guitar Solo B through Guitar Solo C to practice rapidly hitting the red snare with both one and two hands.

## VOCALS

**Percussion:** Yes
**Notes:** The cadence might throw you the first couple of times you sing this, but you should have no trouble keeping the pitch.

## BASS

**Medium:** Don't worry if you're not familiar with this song; just keep the beat and you'll do fine.
**Hard:** Outros A, B, and C are pretty tough, so practice to ensure you don't fail during the homestretch.

## BAND AID

This song is difficult and relatively long. If you're gonna play it on Hard, make sure you have extremely competent players on the guitar and drums.

59

# "ELECTRIC VERSION"— THE NEW PORNOGRAPHERS

## BACKGROUND

**Album:** Electric Version

**Released:** May 6, 2003

**Song Length:** 2:53

**Vocals:** Carl Newman

**Guitar:** Carl Newman, Todd Fancey

**Bass:** John Collins

**Drums:** Kurt Dahle

| DEVELOPER'S TOP SCORES | |
|---|---|
| Bass | 28,629 |
| Drums | 166,775 |
| Guitar | 3,603,799 |
| Vocals | 10,327,087 |
| Band | 1,147,337 |

The New Pornographers' founder, Carl Newman, claims that the band did NOT choose their name in response to Jimmy Swaggart's assertion that music was "the new pornography."

The New Pornographers once played in New York as part of an Independence Day celebration. Nobody seemed to mind that they were Canadian.

## REHEARSAL

| Difficulty Ranking | | | | |
|---|---|---|---|---|
| Difficulty | Drums | Bass | Guitar | Vocals |
| Medium | ★★★ | ★ | ★★ | ★★★✦ |
| Hard | ★★ | ★ | ★★★ | |

### GUITAR

**Solo:** No

**Medium:** Rapid-fire triplets, fast chord transitions, and sustained notes make this is a perfect warm-up for intermediate bassists.

**Hard:** This song will humble you very quickly if you can't accurately shift your hand up and down the fret board.

Practice this technique in order to pull off this song on Hard: Place your index and ring finger on red/blue. Then drop your middle finger and lift your index finger to play yellow/blue. Then slide (no lifting) your middle and ring finger to red/yellow. Finally, lift your middle finger, drop your index finger, and end on green/yellow.

### DRUMS

**Medium:** A new take on the standard drum beat. Practice Verse 3 through Verse 4 to get the hang of using your left hand to hit the alternating red and yellow notes.

**Hard:** The kick drum alternates from every other beat during the verses to every beat during the choruses. This is sure to give less-experienced drummers problems.

### VOCALS

**Percussion:** No

**Notes:** Familiarity with this song helps a lot. Best practice it before playing it with the band.

### BASS

**Medium:** Practice Chorus 1 through Chorus 1A.

**Hard:** Rehearse Chorus 3 through Chorus 3A until you are comfortable playing the rapid high-to-low step-progressions. Practice Verse 1 through Verse 2 until you nail the series of alternating green and red notes (remember to keep your index finger planted on the red note).

## BAND AID

It's hard to say who'll have the most problems with this song if all members select Hard difficulty. Better safe than sorry is a good motto, at least until you've run through it a couple times and judged your aptitude.

61

# "ENTER SANDMAN"— METALLICA

## BACKGROUND

**Album:** Metallica

**Released:** August 12, 1991

**Song Length:** 5:31

**Vocals:** James Hetfield

**Guitar:** Kirk Hammett

**Bass:** Jason Newsted

**Drums:** Lars Ulrich

### DEVELOPER'S TOP SCORES

| | |
|---|---|
| Bass | 202,483 |
| Drums | 351,575 |
| Guitar | 332,399 |
| Vocals | 6,304,420 |
| Band | 1,663,138 |

Metallica was the biggest-selling rock band of the 1990s.

Before meeting singer/guitarist James Hetfield, Lars Ulrich had planned to become a professional tennis player.

James Hetfield has reportedly stated that Aerosmith was his biggest musical influence.

## REHEARSAL

### Difficulty Ranking

| Difficulty | Drums | Bass | Guitar | Vocals |
|---|---|---|---|---|
| Medium | ★★ | ★ | ★★★ | ★★★ |
| Hard | ★★ | ★ | ★★★ | |

## GUITAR

**Solo:** Yes

**Medium:** You better have nimble fingers, because there are a lot of rapid transitions in this song. First things first, though: You must nail Kirk's blistering guitar solo, so practice Guitar Solo A through Guitar Solo D.

**Hard:** The track is so populated with notes during this song that it looks like a candy factory exploded. Don't panic; just learn it piece by piece. Start with the entire intro, though, or you won't last one minute on stage.

## DRUMS

**Medium:** Practice the Outro, Prayer, and Intro. The rest is pretty standard.

**Hard:** Practice Guitar Solo D through the Bridge and end your rehearsal with the Outro.

## VOCALS

**Percussion:** No

**Notes:** A pretty evenly pitched vocal track but if you're suffering, the prayer is all talking, so you'll have a chance to get yourself back into the crowd's favor.

## BASS

**Medium:** There's no part of this song that will cause an intermediate bassist to stumble.

**Hard:** Practice Chorus 1 to test your command of the entire fret board and see if you can't hit those hammer-ons as well.

## BAND AID

Hand bass duties over to the new guy so your skilled players can concentrate on guitar and drums. The vocals are evenly pitched, and the talking "prayer" midway through will save drowning souls.

# "EPIC"—FAITH NO MORE

| DEVELOPER'S TOP SCORES | |
|---|---|
| Bass | 103,253 |
| Drums | 328,475 |
| Guitar | 2,471,239 |
| Vocals | 10,856,539 |
| Band | 1,249,445 |

## BACKGROUND

**Album:** The Real Thing

**Released:** June 20, 1989

**Song Length:** 4:51

**Vocals:** Mike Patton, Chuck Mosley

**Guitar:** Jim Martin

**Bass:** Bill Gould

**Drums:** Mike Bordin

Faith No More singer Mike Patton has also lent his vocals to numerous other bands, including Mr. Bungle, The Dillinger Escape Plan, and Peeping Tom.

After Mike "The Man" Morris left the band, "Faith No Man" became "Faith No More."

## REHEARSAL

| Difficulty Ranking | | | | |
|---|---|---|---|---|
| Difficulty | Drums | Bass | Guitar | Vocals |
| Medium | ★★ | ★ | ★★★ | ★⌐ |
| Hard | ★★ | ★ | ★★★ | |

### GUITAR

**Solo:** No
**Medium:** Select Bridge and practice keeping your finger firmly pressed on the red fret while playing the alternating red and yellow notes.
**Hard:** Practice Bridge 1 all the way through Bridge 2 so when you're performing, you nail the guitar solo and the heavy guitar riff.

Practice Guitar Solo D until you successfully hit 19 notes with a single strum! Now that's talent.

### DRUMS

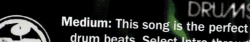

**Medium:** This song is the perfect tempo to practice intermediate drum beats. Select Intro through Verse 1 to practice the kick/high-hat/snare combo or select Guitar Solo A through Guitar Solo D to rehearse the kick/snare/cymbal combo.
**Hard:** The prevalent kick drum only gets more difficult as the song progresses. Practice Bridge 4 to see if you can keep up.

### VOCALS

**Percussion:** Yes
**Notes:** The gradual step-up in pitch may make you falter, but the long section of talking will allow you to regain your composure.

No goldfish died in the making of this chapter.

### BASS

**Medium:** It's possible to play this entire song with one finger. Seriously. Challenge yourself and play Bill Gould's awesome bass line on Hard.
**Hard:** Don't let the song's beginning lull you into a false sense of security. Come the guitar solo, you'll be wishing you ignored our advice and stuck with Medium difficulty.

## BAND AID

It pays to know your skill level when selecting this song's difficulty level. On Hard, the guitar solo will wreak havoc on less-than-skilled guitarists. However, Medium difficulty might be too easy. The vocal track is filled with talking parts that will bail out any struggling singer.

# "FLIRTIN' WITH DISASTER"— MOLLY HATCHET

## DEVELOPER'S TOP SCORES

| Bass | 112,736 |
|------|---------|
| Drums | 202,500 |
| Guitar | 195,677 |
| Vocals | 10,108,891 |
| Band | 9,117,902 |

## BACKGROUND

**Album:** Flirtin' with Disaster

**Released:** 1979

**Song Length:** 4:58

**Vocals:** Danny Joe Brown

**Guitar:** Dave Hlubek, Steve Holland, Duane Roland

**Bass:** Banner Thomas

**Drums:** Bruce Crum

Most of Molly Hatchet's album covers feature Vikings in various forms of combat, including one astride a unicorn destroying a kraken.

Molly Hatchet is named after a mythical Southern prostitute who allegedly beheaded her clients.

## REHEARSAL

### Difficulty Ranking

| Difficulty | Drums | Bass | Guitar | Vocals |
|-----------|-------|------|--------|--------|
| Medium | ★★★ | ★ | ★★ | ★★★✦ |
| Hard | ★★ | ★ | ★★★ | |

# GUITAR

**Solo:** Yes

**Medium:** The solo is very lengthy and moves pretty fast. Make sure you practice it so you're prepared when you play it with a band.

**Hard:** You must have absolutely remarkable control over the entire fret board in order to succeed at this song. The notes move from high to low and back again almost faster than you can see. Check out the Guitar Solo if you're up for a challenge.

# DRUMS

**Medium:** This is a fun song for intermediate drummers. Practice Chorus 2A through the Guitar Break to master the fills.

**Hard:** Attempt this song if you want to practice the intermittent double kick drum. The tempo is very fast, so you might want to slow it down in order to catch the rhythm.

# VOCALS

**Percussion:** Yes

**Notes:** The evenness of the pitch throughout the song makes it a bit easier to get through than other songs of the same difficulty.

# BASS

**Medium:** Select Chorus 2 and practice your hammer-ons and pull-offs.

**Hard:** Practice Chorus 1 until you can rapidly and smoothly move your fingers from green to orange and back again.

# BAND AID

Like many of the advanced songs, this one is more difficult than the Medium or Hard difficulty level suggests. The good news is that intermediate and advanced players will not be bored while attempting Medium and Hard, respectively.

# "FOREPLAY/LONG TIME"— BOSTON

### DEVELOPER'S TOP SCORES

| DEVELOPER'S TOP SCORES | |
|---|---|
| Bass | 200,816 |
| Drums | 242,225 |
| Guitar | 4,309,669 |
| Vocals | 18,277,580 |
| Band | 25,229,360 |

## BACKGROUND

**Album:** Boston

**Released:** August 8, 1976

**Song Length:** 7:47

**Vocals:** Brad Delp

**Guitar:** Barry Goudreau

**Bass:** Tom Scholz

**Drums:** Sib Hashian

Tom Scholz did not start playing guitar until he was 21 and recorded "Foreplay" a year later.

"Foreplay" was reportedly the first piece of music that Tom Scholz ever wrote.

BIG ROCK ENDING!

## REHEARSAL

### Difficulty Ranking

| Difficulty | Drums | Bass | Guitar | Vocals |
|---|---|---|---|---|
| Medium | ★★★ | ★ | ★★ | ★★★★★ |
| Hard | ★★★ | ★ | ★₂ | |

## GUITAR

**Solo:** Yes
**Medium:** There are a few guitar leads and solos in this song but none are terribly difficult.
**Hard:** Select Loud Part 1 to practice transitioning quickly between chords. You must learn to move deftly from adjacent frets to distant frets, so slow the tempo down a bit until you get the rhythm.

## DRUMS

**Medium:** You'll know very quickly whether you're in over your head. This is not a song for intermediate drummers, regardless of the difficulty rating.
**Hard:** Practice Loud Part 1 until you master the red kick/green combo.

## VOCALS

**Percussion:** Yes
**Notes:** This is a tough one for singers without command of the higher pitches. It's got a steep learning curve, so don't be afraid to fail.

## BASS

**Medium:** While your guitarist is trying to keep up with the crazy leads and solos, you're simply laying down a basic rhythm. Practice Outro A through Outro C for more of a challenge.
**Hard:** Practice Loud Part 1 through Quiet Part 2 in addition to Outro A through Outro C to nail the hardest parts of the song.

# BAND AID

Assign your best player to the drums. Both the guitarist and the drummer should choose Medium difficulty unless they have previously practiced harder difficulty levels. A good bassist can take on Hard but might consider the easier road in order to bail out fallen band members.

# "GIMME SHELTER"— ROLLING STONES

## BACKGROUND

**Album:** Let It Bleed

**Released:** December 5, 1969

**Song Length:** 4:32

**Vocals:** Mick Jagger

**Guitar:** Keith Richards

**Bass:** Bill Wyman

**Drums:** Charlie Watts

| DEVELOPER'S TOP SCORES | |
|---|---|
| Bass | 101,819 |
| Drums | 286,400 |
| Guitar | 3,425,599 |
| Vocals | 375,000 |
| Band | 7,989,302 |

**NIFTY**

Keith Richards was reportedly expelled from school for truancy.

**NIFTY**

The first single released by the Rolling Stones was a cover of Chuck Berry's "Come On" and was not liked by either the press or the Stones themselves.

## REHEARSAL

| Difficulty Ranking | | | | |
|---|---|---|---|---|
| Difficulty | Drums | Bass | Guitar | Vocals |
| Medium | ★★ | ★ | ★★★ | ★★★★ |
| Hard | ★★ | ★ | ★★★ | |

## GUITAR

**Medium:** This is a challenging song. If you get comfortable playing through this on Medium, it's time to make the transition to Hard. Rehearse the intro if you need to work on quick, single-note transitions.

**Hard:** That emptiness you feel after attempting this song is due to the untimely and sudden death of your ego and self-esteem. Suffice to say that you're gonna need to slow this one down in order to master it.

## DRUMS

**Medium:** Extremely basic and repetitive drum beat that will only challenge first-timers.

**Hard:** Intermediate drummers will have no problem playing this song on Hard difficulty. The only surprises appear between Outro and Outro B.

## VOCALS

**Percussion:** Yes

**Notes:** An intermediate singer should be able to hold their own on this song.

Put that cocky band member or arrogant friend in his place by challenging him to play this song on Hard.

## BASS

**Medium:** A decent player should have no problem with this bass line. Use your downtime during the intro to laugh at the merciless pounding your guitar player is taking and his futile effort to hang on for dear life.

**Hard:** Select Verse 1 to practice hitting quick progressions.

# BAND AID

Make sure you have a highly skilled guitarist or you're leaving the gig early. Any apprentice drummer or bass player can handle this song on Medium, which is good because they'll most likely need to revive the fallen guitarist.

71

# "GO WITH THE FLOW"— QUEENS OF THE STONE AGE

## BACKGROUND

**Album:** Songs for the Deaf

**Released:** August 27, 2002

**Song Length:** 3:07

**Vocals:** Josh Homme, Nick Oliveri

**Guitar:** Josh Homme

**Bass:** Nick Oliveri

**Drums:** Dave Grohl, Gene Trautmann

| DEVELOPER'S TOP SCORES | |
|---|---|
| Bass | 139,086 |
| Drums | 145,925 |
| Guitar | 3,249,181 |
| Vocals | 10,098,694 |
| Band | 1,585,108 |

At last count, over 25 different musicians have performed in Queens of the Stone Age.

In 2001, former Queens of the Stone Age member Nick Oliveri was arrested in Rio for performing onstage wearing only his bass.

## REHEARSAL

| Difficulty Ranking | | | | |
|---|---|---|---|---|
| Difficulty | Drums | Bass | Guitar | Vocals |
| Medium | ★★ | ★ | ★★★ | ★★★★★ |
| Hard | ★★ | ★ | ★★★ | |

## GUITAR

**Solo:** No
**Medium:** Select the chorus and practice strumming both up and down.
**Hard:** If you have trouble double-shifting your fingers from green/yellow to yellow/orange, this is the song to practice on. Play the chorus until you get the hang of it.

## DRUMS

**Medium:** A basic beat but the transitions from red/yellow to yellow/blue to red/green during the chorus are fun to pull off.
**Hard:** Only the most experienced should attempt. Even at 70 percent speed, you'll still wish you had a second kick drum pedal to help you keep up.

## VOCALS

**Percussion:** No
**Notes:** A solid song for an intermediate to practice both high-pitched notes and falling tones.

## BASS

**Medium:** There are a few spots during the chorus that might trip up beginners, but overall the song is pretty easy.
**Hard:** Even seasoned bass players may stumble during the rapid progressions within Verse 2.

### RIFF

To learn the effective use of a hammer-on, players of all abilities will benefit from practicing Verse 2 at half-speed. If successful, you'll hit several notes with a single strum.

### FILL

On Hard, grip the strum bar lightly between your thumb and forefinger and strum up and down rapidly to hit every note.

## BAND AID

For the drummer, hard means hard, so don't bite off more than you can chew and bring the band down with you. The bassist and the guitarist should heed that advice as well, although their tracks are a bit more forgiving.

# "GREEN GRASS AND HIGH TIDES"— *AS MADE FAMOUS BY* THE OUTLAWS *

## DETAILS ON THE CLASSIC

**Album:** Outlaws

**Released:** 1975

**Song Length:** 9:49

**Vocals:** Hughie Thomasson, Billy Jones, Henry Paul

**Guitar:** Hughie Thomasson, Billy Jones, Henry Paul

**Bass:** Frank O'Keefe

**Drums:** Monte Yoho

| DEVELOPER'S TOP SCORES | |
| --- | --- |
| Bass | 276,258 |
| Drums | 715,992 |
| Guitar | 790,763 |
| Vocals | 10,531,918 |
| Band | 3,670,636 |

The Outlaws' singer and guitarist Hughie Thomasson defined the band's signature Southern sound with his impressive and influential guitar skills. Thomasson also later played as a member of Lynyrd Skynyrd in the '90s.

BIG ROCK ENDING!

This 1975 hit by The Outlaws is entitled "Green Grass and High Tides." The 1966 greatest-hits album by the Rolling Stones is entitled "High Tide and Green Grass." Try not to get confused.

## REHEARSAL

| Difficulty Ranking | | | | |
| --- | --- | --- | --- | --- |
| Difficulty | Drums | Bass | Guitar | Vocals |
| Medium | ★★★ | ★ | ★★ | ★★★♪ |
| Hard | ★★★ | ★ | ★★ | |

* This is a cover version of a song made famous by the artist indicated.

## GUITAR

**Solo:** Yes
**Medium:** This song boasts the longest solo in the game, some 700 notes! It's a battle against fatigue more than anything else, however. Instead, practice Intro Fast.
**Hard:** The good news about this song is that you'll know real fast if you can cut it. Get through Intro Fast and you're on your way. All that's left is an upswing in the already-fast tempo followed by a thousand-note (give or take) solo. Have fun!

Nail this solo and you are required by law to smash your guitar into the stage. Furthermore, the band member with the lowest score has to buy you a new one.

## DRUMS

**Medium:** This is a long song, but the beats are nothing new. If you have the stamina, have at it.
**Hard:** This song's sheer length in addition to all the changes and tempo swings make it extremely hard to play. Most of the song is comprised of standard beats, but the chorus and parts of the guitar solos are nightmares.

## VOCALS

**Percussion:** Yes
**Notes:** This is a tough song; you'll need a lot of range to pull it off. Don't let the song's length discourage you; most of it is guitar solos.

## BASS

**Medium:** Before attempting this one, select Fast Part through Guitar Solo 2B and see if you can keep up.
**Hard:** You best be a pro at hammer-ons or you won't survive very long once the song kicks into high gear.

## BAND AID

This is a marathon of a song, but it's extremely fun for guitarists due to the epic solos. On Medium, the song is playable by experienced musicians, but Hard is a different story—it takes rock band pros to pull it off.

# "HERE IT GOES AGAIN"— OK GO

## BACKGROUND

**Album:** Oh No

**Released:** September 25, 2006

**Song Length:** 2:59

**Vocals:** Damian Kulash Jr.

**Guitar:** Damian Kulash Jr.

**Bass:** Timothy Nordwind

**Drums:** Dan Konopka

| DEVELOPER'S TOP SCORES | |
|---|---|
| Bass | 108,030 |
| Drums | 175,880 |
| Guitar | 2,878,129 |
| Vocals | 8,600,131 |
| Band | 3,851,513 |

OK Go's singer Damian Kulash and bassist Tim Nordwind reportedly met at summer camp as children.

BIG ROCK ENDING!

The members of OK Go have an imaginary robot named Jorge.

## REHEARSAL

| Difficulty Ranking | | | | |
|---|---|---|---|---|
| Difficulty | Drums | Bass | Guitar | Vocals |
| Medium | ★★★ | ★ | ★★ | ★♪ |
| Hard | ★★★ | ★ | ★★ | |

## GUITAR

**Solo:** Yes

**Medium:** Practice the bridge—it's actually the guitar solo. And remember to shift your index finger to the red fret.

**Hard:** "Just when you think you're in control…just when you think you're on a roll," they throw a red/blue at you! This is a tough one. You're gonna use the entire fret board in almost all combinations. Practice the chorus at a slower speed until you get the hang of the progression.

## DRUMS

**Medium:** If you need to learn how to lay down a steady intermediate rhythm, practice Verse 3 through Chorus 3.

**Hard:** Practice Chorus 3 through the outro.

Remember, during practice, you are free to focus on one drum at a time. On Hard, it might help to start with the kick drum and then add the high hat/snare when comfortable.

## VOCALS

**Percussion:** No

**Notes:** The song gets tougher after the solo, so save your overdrive in case you start to falter.

## BASS

**Medium:** The few blue notes that appear are during the bridge; practice it if you have trouble hitting notes that high.

**Hard:** Practice Verse 1A to get the hang of quickly shifting your index finger to the red fret in order to hit the orange notes.

## BAND AID

Even intermediate bassists can handle their own on Hard difficulty. The guitarist and the drummer both have their work cut out for them if playing the song on Hard, so if unfamiliar with the song, it's best to start those instruments on Medium.

# ROCKBAND

# "HIGHWAY STAR"— DEEP PURPLE

## BACKGROUND

**Album:** Machine Head

**Released:** May 1972

**Song Length:** 6:05

**Vocals:** Ian Gillan

**Guitar:** Ritchie Blackmore

**Bass:** Roger Glover

**Drums:** Ian Paice

| DEVELOPER'S TOP SCORES | |
|---|---|
| Bass | 225,796 |
| Drums | 272,800 |
| Guitar | 328,340 |
| Vocals | 12,396,979 |
| Band | 20,603,188 |

Deep Purple reportedly improvised "Highway Star" on their tour bus on the way to a show after a journalist asked them about their songwriting process.

BIG ROCK ENDING!

As a member of Deep Purple, Ritchie Blackmore was one of the most influential guitarists in rock 'n' roll. He also has an awesome mustache.

## REHEARSAL

| Difficulty Ranking | | | | |
|---|---|---|---|---|
| Difficulty | Drums | Bass | Guitar | Vocals |
| Medium | ★★★ | ★ | ★★ | ★★★★★ |
| Hard | ★★★ | ★ | ★★ | |

## GUITAR

**Solo:** Yes

**Medium:** This serves as your crash course in consecutive note-playing. Select the Intro and do your best to hit every note in the stream (we lost count at like 28,432). Remember to strum up and down or your hand is gonna hurt!

**Hard:** Welcome to the craziest guitar solo in the game. It contains over 250 hammer-ons and pull-offs! Nail 'em all and your place in the pantheon of shredders is assured.

## DRUMS

**Medium:** Practice Chorus 1 to get the red kick/green timing down.

**Hard:** Seasoned drummers only, but less-experienced players might want to give the Intro a shot to see just how fast and how long they can pound that snare.

## VOCALS

**Percussion:** Yes

**Notes:** Use the long opening note to find the correct pitch. Also, it's better to have unspent energy after the song than to need it and not have it—conserve it until you learn the song.

## BASS

**Medium:** As with the guitar composition, you'll be playing long streams of consecutive notes. Select Guitar Solo D for a quick lesson.

**Hard:** Think bassists have it easy? Well, Verse 1 through Chorus 1 will change your mind. Slow it down a bit in order to get a grip on the progression.

## BAND AID

Every member should select Medium difficulty or they're gonna fail very quickly. Leave Hard for those who've spent a lot of time rehearsing.

# "I GET BY"—HONEST BOB AND THE FACTORY-TO-DEALER INCENTIVES

## BACKGROUND

**Album:** Second & Eighteen

**Released:** —

**Song Length:** 4:17

**Vocals:** Dan Schmidt, Greg Huang

**Guitar:** Chris Rigopulos

**Bass:** Greg Huang

**Drums:** Bill Foster

| DEVELOPER'S TOP SCORES | |
|---|---|
| Bass | 111,749 |
| Drums | 5,983,561 |
| Guitar | 200,612 |
| Vocals | 15,667,246 |
| Band | 1,088,708 |

None of the members of Honest Bob and the Factory-to-Dealer Incentives is named Bob, although they are all scrupulously honest.

Yes, that is an F-sharp bar being played during the words "F-sharp bar."

## REHEARSAL

| Difficulty Ranking | | | | |
|---|---|---|---|---|
| Difficulty | Drums | Bass | Guitar | Vocals |
| Medium | ★★★ | ★ | ★★ | ★★★★★ |
| Hard | ★★★ | ★ | ★★ | |

## GUITAR

**Solo:** No
**Medium:** Select Speed Up A and B and practice hitting the hammer-ons and pull-offs.
**Hard:** There's a tough but fun series of chord transitions in Chorus 1.

## DRUMS

**Medium:** The constant kick drum will give many average drummers problems. If you can handle that, then practice the Bridge and you're home free.
**Hard:** The faster tempo might be easier for some drummers to play, so give it a shot even if you haven't yet mastered Medium.

## VOCALS

**Percussion:** Yes
**Notes:** This is one song you should practice before you play. Of course, where is the fun in that? Hope you have some lung capacity, 'cause this one is gonna take the wind outta ya.

## BASS

**Medium:** Nothing too taxing here; you might want to try this song on Hard.
**Hard:** Practice Chorus 1 if you need experience playing the orange fret.

## BAND AID

Feel free to let your bassist and guitarist play above his or her usual difficulty level. However, hand the sticks to an adept drummer, whatever the difficulty level.

# ROCKBAND™

# "I THINK I'M PARANOID"— GARBAGE

## BACKGROUND

**Album:** Version 2.0

**Released:** May 12, 1998

**Length:** 3:38

**Vocals:** Shirley Manson

**Guitar:** Duke Erikson, Steve Marker

**Bass:** Steve Marker

**Drums:** Butch Vig

| DEVELOPER'S TOP SCORES | |
|---|---|
| Bass | 117,754 |
| Drums | 149,575 |
| Guitar | 1,901,593 |
| Vocals | 14,200,858 |
| Band | 3,110,186 |

Shirley Manson calls her iconic orange guitar "Rita."

Garbage cofounder and drummer Butch Vig also happened to produce Nirvana's *Nevermind* and the Smashing Pumpkins' *Gish* and *Siamese Dream*.

## REHEARSAL

| Difficulty Ranking | | | | |
|---|---|---|---|---|
| Difficulty | Drums | Bass | Guitar | Vocals |
| Medium | ★★★ | ★ | ★★ | ★ |
| Hard | ★★ | ★ | ★★★ | |

## GUITAR

**Solo:** No

**Medium:** Play through Chorus 1B and learn to keep your finger firmly on the red fret when you see the alternating red and yellow notes approaching. Then, you need only lift and press with one finger. It might seem pointless, but trust us, as the songs get harder and faster, you'll need that skill.

**Hard:** If you've got chord transitions down but still get tripped up moving up and down the fret board to catch rapidly moving single notes, then this song is great practice.

## DRUMS

**Medium:** This song is the perfect tempo for novice drummers to work on intermediate drum beats. Practice the bridge through the song's end until you've mastered them.

**Hard:** A nice song to practice in order to transition from an intermediate drummer to an experienced one.

Give this song a shot on the harder difficulty levels; you may find that you keep up as good or better with the faster tempo.

## VOCALS

**Percussion:** No

**Notes:** This is a tough song for beginners because the pre-chorus and the chorus are sung at different pitches.

## BASS

**Medium:** Play the Main Riff through Verse 2 and practice keeping your finger planted firmly on the lowest note—first on red and then on green.

**Hard:** Practice Chorus 1A if you're having problems moving from the green fret to the blue fret. Practice the Main Riff if you need to sharpen your ability to hit the orange notes.

## BAND AID

If you want to play on Hard, put your best player on the guitar. Anyone with moderate experience can pick up the repetitive and fairly straightforward drum beat. Your singer should have range or you may need to bail them out, even on Medium.

# "I'M SO SICK"—FLYLEAF

## BACKGROUND

**Album:** Flyleaf

**Released:** October 4, 2005

**Song Length:** 2:55

**Vocals:** Lacey Mosley

**Guitar:** Sameer Bhattacharya, Jared Hartmann

**Bass:** Pat Seals

**Drums:** James Culpepper

| DEVELOPER'S TOP SCORES | |
|---|---|
| Bass | 207,859 |
| Drums | 103,360 |
| Guitar | 169,576 |
| Vocals | 4,761,406 |
| Band | 557,960 |

Flyleaf was originally called "Passerby," but in a longstanding rock tradition, another band had already claimed the name.

## REHEARSAL

### Difficulty Ranking

| Difficulty | Drums | Bass | Guitar | Vocals |
|---|---|---|---|---|
| Medium | ★ | ★★ | ★★★ | ★★★★★ |
| Hard | ★★ | ★ | ★★★ | |

## GUITAR

**Solo:** No

**Medium:** Play through Chorus 2 until you get the hang of the chord transitions. Then select the Bridge through Chorus 3 for a tougher challenge.

**Hard:** Select the Outro so you can crush the difficult riff that appears throughout the song. You might want to slow it down a bit to get the progression down.

## DRUMS

**Medium:** The slow tempo and standard beat make this an excellent song for a beginner to try their hand at Medium.

**Hard:** The verses are the hardest parts of this song. If you're capable of handling those, the rest of the song should pose no problems.

## VOCALS

**Percussion:** No

**Notes:** The steep rises in pitch will cause trouble for both novice and seasoned vocalists alike.

## BASS

**Medium:** Practice Chorus 1 until you hit every note in the series; your score in the Solo and Band World Tour depends on it.

**Hard:** Select the Outro to work on your dexterity. It's a good exercise in moving quickly from one end of the fret board to the other.

## BAND AID

The song is meant to be played on Hard. Anything easier and the tempo doesn't match the song's energy. However, if your group is used to Medium, you'll all have to practice a bit to keep up.

85

# "IN BLOOM"—NIRVANA

## BACKGROUND

**Album:** Nevermind

**Released:** October 1992

**Song Length:** 4:14

**Vocals:** Kurt Cobain

**Guitar:** Kurt Cobain

**Bass:** Krist Novoselic

**Drums:** Dave Grohl

### DEVELOPER'S TOP SCORES

| | |
|---|---|
| Bass | 99,702 |
| Drums | 212,475 |
| Guitar | 317,528 |
| Vocals | 16,846,532 |
| Band | 9,849,116 |

## REHEARSAL

### Difficulty Ranking

| Difficulty | Drums | Bass | Guitar | Vocals |
|---|---|---|---|---|
| Medium | ★★★ | ★ | ★★ | ♪ |
| Hard | ★★★ | ★ | ★★ | |

## GUITAR

**Solo:** Yes
**Medium:** Practice Chorus 1B to go from red/yellow to green/red to single yellows to single reds while never once lifting your middle finger from the red fret.
**Hard:** Practice Intro A through Intro B; there's lots of shifting your hand up and down the frets to hit the varied power chords.

If you're not very good at shifting your hands on the frets, practicing the chorus on Hard will help immensely.

## DRUMS

**Medium:** If we had to pick one song to teach beginner/intermediate drumming, this would be it. Practice Chorus 1A through Chorus 1B to build a solid foundation.
**Hard:** Give Intro B some attention to see if you can master the double kick drum. Also, repeat the chorus until you can nail every kick-drum note and the intermittent yellow notes.

While playing the chorus, practice counting to yourself: 1,2,3,4,1,2,3,4.... On every beat, hit the yellow high hat. Then, on every 3 strike, the red snare. Finally, add a kick on every 1.

Remember, in Practice mode, you can slow the song down until you get the hang of the rhythm.

## VOCALS

**Percussion:** No
**Notes:** The chorus requires a consistently high pitch, so practice it if you're having trouble.

## BASS

**Medium:** Very easy and simple bass line. Only a few blue keys and they fall at the chorus' end.
**Hard:** Practice Bridge 3 to get the hang of hammer-ons and pull-offs.

# BAND AID

On Medium, the guitar and bass players can relax but the drummer has some steady work to do. All three will earn their pay on Hard, and a good drummer is a must. The vocals are pretty straightforward; even a novice player can pick up the intonations.

# "LEARN TO FLY"— FOO FIGHTERS

## BACKGROUND

**Album:** There Is Nothing Left to Lose

**Released:** November 9, 1999

**Song Length:** 3:55

**Vocals:** Dave Grohl

**Guitar:** Dave Grohl

**Bass:** Nate Mendel

**Drums:** Taylor Hawkins

| DEVELOPER'S TOP SCORES | |
|---|---|
| Bass | 41,553 |
| Drums | 135,025 |
| Guitar | 3,307,690 |
| Vocals | 14,251,546 |
| Band | 2,599,386 |

Dave Grohl played all of the instruments (save for one guitar part) on the Foo Fighters' debut record.

The Foo Fighters are named after a WWII term for an unidentified flying object.

## REHEARSAL

| Difficulty Ranking | | | | |
|---|---|---|---|---|
| Difficulty | Drums | Bass | Guitar | Vocals |
| Medium | ★★★ | ★ | ★★ | ★ |
| Hard | ★★★ | ★ | ★★ | |

## GUITAR

**Solo:** No
**Medium:** Practice Chorus 3 and the bridge.
**Hard:** Practice Verse 1 through Chorus 1.

Remember, in order to hit single notes between two chords, you can leave your finger on the lower note and simply raise and lower the finger on the higher note.

## DRUMS

**Medium:** A standard intermediate beat, but tackle Verse 1 through Verse 2 to master the nuances of the drum track.
**Hard:** If this song is giving you trouble, then practice Chorus 2 and ignore the kick drum. Once you find the rhythm with your hands, work in your feet.

## VOCALS

**Percussion:** No
**Notes:** Watch your pitch during the chorus, especially if you tend to err on the high side.

## BASS

**Medium:** Play through Chorus 4 to practice hitting long strings of consecutive notes.
**Hard:** Practice Chorus 2 to increase your skill at hitting intermittent groupings of notes.

## BAND AID

You'll need a decent drummer, even on Medium difficulty. The bassist can be a novice, as long as he or she is familiar with the song. The guitarist should stick to Medium unless well practiced. An inexperienced singer should stick to Medium difficulty at most.

89

# "MAIN OFFENDER"— THE HIVES

## BACKGROUND

**Album:** Veni Vidi Vicious

**Released:** April 10, 2000

**Song Length:** 2:33

**Vocals:** Pelle Almqvist

**Guitar:** Nicholaus Arson, Vigilante Carlstroem

**Bass:** Dr. Matt Destruction

**Drums:** Chris Dangerous

| DEVELOPER'S TOP SCORES | |
|---|---|
| Bass | 46,285 |
| Drums | 104,075 |
| Guitar | 2,365,210 |
| Vocals | 6,087,610 |
| Band | 719,648 |

The Hives hail from a very small town in Sweden called "Fagersta."

The Hives allegedly have a songwriter and Svengali named Randy Fitzsimmons who has never been interviewed and is rumored not to exist.

## REHEARSAL

| Difficulty Ranking | | | | |
|---|---|---|---|---|
| Difficulty | Drums | Bass | Guitar | Vocals |
| Medium | ★★★ | ★ | ★★ | ★★✦ |
| Hard | ★★★ | ★ | ★★ | |

## GUITAR

**Solo:** Yes
**Medium:** The first solo comes up right after the intro and requires some fast strumming.
**Hard:** Verse 2 is going to test your ability to quickly move from green/yellow to yellow/orange and then back to red.

## DRUMS

**Medium:** Basic red/blue/kick pattern with a twist at the end. Rehearse Guitar Hook 2 through the ending to pick it up.
**Hard:** Practice hitting the rapid kick-drum notes at the end of Chorus 2.

## VOCALS

**Percussion:** Yes
**Notes:** Many of the notes drop off to a lower pitch, which may cause less-experienced singers to stumble. If you've hit them before, though, this song is a drop in the hat.

## BASS

**Medium:** Nothing too taxing here for the intermediate bassist.
**Hard:** Select Verse 3 through Verse 4 to practice sliding your pinky from the blue fret to the orange fret and then back again.

# BAND AID

Experienced bassists should play this on Hard, as should fast-fingered guitarists. The vocals aren't terribly daunting, but the drums on Hard are.

# "MAPS"—YEAH YEAH YEAHS

| DEVELOPER'S TOP SCORES ||
|---|---|
| Bass | 65,161 |
| Drums | 272,120 |
| Guitar | 1,696,168 |
| Vocals | 9,285,508 |
| Band | 12,003,554 |

## BACKGROUND

**Album:** Fever to Tell

**Released:** February 10, 2004

**Song Length:** 3:34

**Vocals:** Karen O

**Guitar:** Nick Zinner

**Drums:** Brian Chase

Formed in 2000 in Brooklyn, the Yeah Yeah Yeahs get their band name from a phrase commonly heard among impatient New Yorkers.

Karen O is notorious for her constantly changing, often outlandish stage wardrobe.

## REHEARSAL

| Difficulty Ranking |||||
|---|---|---|---|---|
| Difficulty | Drums | Bass | Guitar | Vocals |
| Medium | ★★★ | ★ | ★★ | ♪ |
| Hard | ★★★ | ★ | ★★ | |

## GUITAR

**Solo:** No
**Medium:** A very steady rhythm but nothing too challenging.
**Hard:** Practice Guitar Line 2, but be warned, it's tough. Remember, only the highest note counts, so keep the lower frets pressed to minimize movement and maximize efficiency.

Beginners should practice the chorus on Hard to get the hang of rapidly playing consecutively higher and then lower notes.

## DRUMS

**Medium:** Bridge 2 is the hardest part of the song.
**Hard:** The constant kick drum makes this a fun song to play, but practice Bridge 1 or your band will be looking for another drummer.

## VOCALS

**Percussion:** Yes
**Notes:** Hope you can hold a note, 'cause the chorus requires it. Fortunately, the verses are easier to ace.

## BASS

**Medium:** Long periods of inactivity and a slow but steady beat make this the song to play when you need to grab a drink!
**Hard:** Practice Bridge 1 to get the hang of fast strumming.

# BAND AID

Your bassist could've just returned from a month-long bender and yet still pull this off. The second guitar line on Hard is, well, hard, but overall the drummer is the one who makes or breaks you on this song. Grab a singer who has practiced this song before and you'll be fine.

# "MISSISSIPPI QUEEN"—
### AS MADE FAMOUS BY MOUNTAIN *

## DETAILS ON THE CLASSIC

**Album:** Climbing!
**Released:** May 1970
**Song Length:** 2:30
**Vocals:** Leslie West
**Guitar:** Leslie West
**Bass:** Felix Pappalardi
**Drums:** Corky Laing

| DEVELOPER'S TOP SCORES | |
| --- | --- |
| Bass | 61,123 |
| Drums | 140,760 |
| Guitar | 1,077,220 |
| Vocals | 5,402,233 |
| Band | 6,985,343 |

It is rumored that "Mississippi Queen" was spontaneously written by drummer Corky Laing during a power outage in a club on Nantucket and was inspired by a nubile vacationer.

Ozzy Osbourne covered "Mississippi Queen" on his 2005 album *Under Cover*.

## REHEARSAL

| Difficulty Ranking | | | | |
| --- | --- | --- | --- | --- |
| Difficulty | Drums | Bass | Guitar | Vocals |
| Medium | ★★★ | ★ | ★★ | ★★★★ |
| Hard | ★★★ | ★ | ★★ | |

\* This is a cover version of a song made famous by the artist indicated.

## GUITAR

**Solo:** Yes
**Medium:** Fairly straightforward but practice Verse 1A through Verse 1B to get the hang of quickly strumming a bunch of consecutive notes.
**Hard:** Practice Verse 1A through Verse 1B to master moving from red/blue to yellow/orange and back again.

During Verse 1A and Verse 1B on Hard, your index finger should be on the red fret before shifting to the yellow fret. You'll have time before Verse 1C kicks in to shift your index finger back to the home position (green fret).

## DRUMS

**Medium:** Practice Verse 1C through Verse 2A to have some fun with the kick drum.
**Hard:** Practice Verse 1A through Verse 1C to get used to the changes in the kick-drum pattern.

## VOCALS

**Percussion:** Yes
**Notes:** The transition from longer notes to shorter, punctuated ones may trip up singers unfamiliar with the song.

## BASS

**Medium:** Nothing too difficult here; even a beginner should score high.
**Hard:** Practice Verse 1A if you have trouble hitting a red and then a blue note.

## BAND AID

A nice break from the standard song structure, but for inexperienced drummers and guitarists, the tough sections seem to go on and on.

95

# "NIGHTMARE"— CROOKED X

## BACKGROUND

**Album:** (unreleased)

**Released:** N/A

**Song Length:** 4:32

**Vocals:** Forrest

**Guitar:** Jesse

**Bass:** Josh

**Drums:** Boomer

| DEVELOPER'S TOP SCORES | |
|---|---|
| Bass | 91,422 |
| Drums | 167,757 |
| Guitar | 158,015 |
| Vocals | 3,477,970 |
| Band | 543,834 |

To date, Crooked X has played over 85 gigs, despite the fact that all the members are in their early teens.

BIG ROCK ENDING!

## REHEARSAL

| Difficulty Ranking | | | | |
|---|---|---|---|---|
| Difficulty | Drums | Bass | Guitar | Vocals |
| Medium | ★★ | ★ | ★★★ | ★★ |
| Hard | ★★ | ★ | ★★★ | |

## GUITAR

**Solo:** Yes
**Medium:** Select Chorus 1 to try your hand at a few simple step-progressions.
**Hard:** You need to be quick and clean with your chord transitions to survive this one. Play Verse 1 and the Outro until you get the progression. Oh, and we totally understand if you need to slow it down a bit. Really. We do. Hey, maybe my little nephew could help you out?

## DRUMS

**Medium:** Select Verse 2 and practice hitting red/green.
**Hard:** The alternating single and double kick drum will throw most inexperienced drummers, but once you get the hang of it, you'll score well.

## VOCALS

**Percussion:** Yes
**Notes:** Finding the correct pitch on this might take a little trial and error, but by now you're used to that.

## BASS

**Medium:** Thirty percent of the song is a series of continuous green notes. Don't screw 'em up; your score depends on your accuracy. Also, practice the Outro if you need help with simple step-progressions (blue to green).
**Hard:** Verse 1 might trip you up, but even if it doesn't, it's still really fun to play.

If your bassist whines that he never shares the spotlight with the guitarist, remind the wannabe Cliff Burton that the minute he writes anything as cool as the Iron Maidenesque opening riff to this song, he can have center stage—it stings a bit, but it builds character.

# BAND AID

Like most songs in the hard rock and heavy metal genre, this one is meant to be played fast. Practice on Hard so when you take the stage, you feel like you're really playing along.

# "ORANGE CRUSH"—R.E.M.

## DEVELOPER'S TOP SCORES

| | |
|---|---|
| Bass | 72,008 |
| Drums | 201,875 |
| Guitar | 1,707,949 |
| Vocals | 3,415,798 |
| Band | 919,688 |

## BACKGROUND

**Album:** Green
**Released:** November 7, 1988
**Song Length:** 3:51
**Vocals:** Michael Stipe
**Guitar:** Peter Buck
**Bass:** Mike Mills
**Drums:** Bill Berry

In 1998, R.E.M.'s Michael Stipe published a book of his photographs of influential singer/songwriter Patti Smith on tour.

R.E.M. held their first rehearsals in a converted church.

## REHEARSAL

### Difficulty Ranking

| Difficulty | Drums | Bass | Guitar | Vocals |
|---|---|---|---|---|
| Medium | ★★★ | ★ | ★★ | ★♪ |
| Hard | ★★★ | ★ | ★★ | |

## GUITAR

**Solo:** Yes

**Medium:** This won't cause too much trouble, even for the novices. Give Hard a shot!

**Hard:** The only orange notes appear during the solo, so there's little need to shift your hand position. However, practice Chorus 2 through Chorus 3 to master the quick, single-note transitions.

In Hard mode, using the high frets during the solo is ill-advised, as you won't have enough time to transition back to the main frets.

## DRUMS

**Medium:** Practice Chorus 3. If it gives you trouble, run through it a few times without worrying about the kick drum. Once you find the rhythm, add the kick drum.

**Hard:** Chorus 3 will pose a problem to all but the most polished drummers. Play through it at a slower speed to understand the progressions.

## VOCALS

**Percussion:** Yes

**Notes:** The long, high-pitched notes might make novice singers fail.

## BASS

**Medium:** Play through Chorus 2 a few times if you find hitting the blue notes tough.

**Hard:** The rapid single-note transitions throughout Chorus 2 and Chorus 3 are fun to play.

# BAND AID

Experienced bassists and guitarists should be able to handle Hard. Inexperienced drummers and singers should select Easy until they learn the song.

# "OUTSIDE"—TRIBE

## BACKGROUND

**Album:** Here at the Home

**Released:** 1988

**Length:** 4:56

**Vocals:** Janet LaValley

**Guitar:** Eric Brosius

**Bass:** Greg LoPiccolo

**Drummer:** David Penzo

**Keyboards:** Terri Barous

| DEVELOPER'S TOP SCORES | |
|---|---|
| Bass | 87,785 |
| Drums | 347,475 |
| Guitar | 285,128 |
| Vocals | 17,749,216 |
| Band | 1,267,555 |

Tribe had a radio hit in South Africa and continues to make about $2.00 a year from South African airplay royalties.

The members of Tribe recorded their first album (released on vinyl!) in the basement of the house where they all lived in Brighton, Massachusetts.

## REHEARSAL

| Difficulty Ranking | | | | |
|---|---|---|---|---|
| Difficulty | Drums | Bass | Guitar | Vocals |
| Medium | ★★★ | ★ | ★★ | ★★★ |
| Hard | ★★ | ★ | ★★★ | |

## GUITAR

**Solo:** Yes

**Medium:** Practice Chorus 2B to get the hang of several chord transitions.

**Hard:** You've gotta be really good to get through this song. If you need help, practice the first two verses and the choruses until you have it down.

Using the whammy bar during some songs just sounds obnoxious. However, it fits the electric mood of this song perfectly.

## DRUMS

**Medium:** Practice Chant 1, but even if you can't pick it up, don't worry; the rest of the song is the standard snare/high-hat/kick rhythm.

**Hard:** Once you become familiar with playing the song on Medium, try your hands and foot at Hard. It's the same high-hat/snare pattern, but the kick drum is much more prevalent.

## VOCALS

**Percussion:** Yes

**Notes:** This song's melancholy lows and hopeful highs will challenge a novice vocalist, but don't be afraid to sing with energy or you'll miss the point.

## BASS

**Medium:** Practice Chorus 1A to work on your nimbleness.

**Hard:** Select Fast Part through the Ending. It's a long section, but your success depends on dexterity and consistent repetition and stamina.

# BAND AID

Extremely fun and difficult to tackle on Hard, but manageable for intermediate players on Medium.

103

# ROCKBAND

## "PARANOID"—
### AS MADE FAMOUS BY BLACK SABBATH *

### DETAILS ON THE CLASSIC

**Album:** Paranoid

**Released:** September 18, 1970

**Song Length:** 2:52

**Vocals:** Ozzy Osbourne

**Guitar:** Tomi Iommi

**Bass:** Geezer Butler

**Drums:** Bill Ward

| DEVELOPER'S TOP SCORES | |
|---|---|
| Bass | 133,609 |
| Drums | 118,816 |
| Guitar | 146,431 |
| Vocals | 5,741,704 |
| Band | 759,649 |

After leaving Black Sabbath in 1979, Ozzy Osbourne was replaced by Ronnie James Dio, who was replaced by Ian Gillan, who was replaced by David Donato, who was replaced by Glenn Hughes, who was replaced by Ray Gillen, who was replaced by Tony Martin. And so on.

## BIG ROCK ENDING!

While a member of Black Sabbath, Ozzy Osbourne had a fondness for shaving off his bandmates' eyebrows as they slept.

### REHEARSAL

| Difficulty Ranking | | | | |
|---|---|---|---|---|
| Difficulty | Drums | Bass | Guitar | Vocals |
| Medium | ★★★ | ★ | ★★ | ♪ |
| Hard | ★★★ | ★★ | ★ | |

* This is a cover version of a song made famous by the artist indicated.

## GUITAR

**Solo:** Yes

**Medium:** Select Verse 1 through Verse 2 and practice hitting those fast streams of consecutive notes.

**Hard:** Veteran players need only devote their practice time to the guitar solo.

## DRUMS

**Medium:** Nothing surprising here. Keep a steady count and you'll have no problem picking up and keeping the beat.

**Hard:** Good practice for those who can't perform a consistent double kick drum without throwing off their rhythm.

## VOCALS

**Percussion:** No

**Notes:** Don't oversing this one; it takes a steady pitch.

## BASS

**Medium:** This song is a tutorial on consistently hitting long sections of consecutive notes.

**Hard:** Slow down the chorus and practice hitting the long series of hammer-ons.

# BAND AID

It takes a very good drummer to pull off this song in Hard mode. Those guitarists and bassists playing out of their league may find a section or two over their head, but the majority of the song is navigable and repetitive. A novice vocalist can handle the microphone.

# "PLEASURE (PLEASURE)"— BANG CAMARO

| DEVELOPER'S TOP SCORES ||
|---|---|
| Bass | 210,673 |
| Drums | 125,950 |
| Guitar | 203,673 |
| Vocals | 6,908,122 |
| Band | 2,517,649 |

## BACKGROUND

**Album:** Bang Camaro

**Released:** February 2007

**Length:** 3:34

**Vocals:** 18 dudes

**Guitar:** Bryn Bennett, Alex Necochea, Maclaine Diemer

**Bass:** Dave Riley

**Drummer:** Andy Dole

Four out of five female prisoners polled preferred Bang Camaro to a pillow fight.

Just before they cry themselves to sleep, the members of Bang Camaro like to gather around their tour van to discuss their favorite fantasy artwork.

The term "ostinato" refers to a melodic or rhythmic pattern that is repeated persistently. A popular example is the two-note ostinato John Williams uses to build suspense in *Jaws*.

## REHEARSAL

| Difficulty Ranking |||||
|---|---|---|---|---|
| Difficulty | Drums | Bass | Guitar | Vocals |
| Medium | ★★★ | ★ | ★★ | ★ |
| Hard | ★★ | ★ | ★★★ | |

## GUITAR

**Solo:** Yes
**Medium:** The step-progressions at the end of Verse 1 require quick fingers to pull off.
**Hard:** Select Chorus 3 for step-progressions and Guitar Ostinato through Guitar Solo B for, well, you'll see. During the Ostinato, it helps to shift your index finger from green to red to yellow and then back again.

## DRUMS

**Medium:** Nothing but basic rhythms punctuated by fun fills.
**Hard:** There are a few tough sections to navigate, like the end of Verse 3, but overall this is a good song for an intermediate drummer to take on.

Any self-respecting drummer should be twirling his sticks as the Guitar Solo ends and the Break begins. All of the L.A. poseurs are doing it!

## VOCALS

**Percussion:** Yes
**Notes:** How can you not have fun singing this homage to hair metal? Makeup and leather pants tucked into cowboy boots are the dress code, and that's for the men!

## BASS

**Medium:** Select Verse 1 through Verse 1A to practice consistently hitting the flow of consecutive notes.
**Hard:** Practice Verse 2 and see how deftly you can move from one end of the fret board to the other.

## BAND AID

This fun throwback song provides a good opportunity for band members to step up and play at the difficulty level just above their current ability. Each instrument's composition includes at least one difficult section, but overall, you should be able to get through them.

107

# ROCKBAND™

# "REPTILIA"—THE STROKES

## BACKGROUND

**Album:** Room on Fire

**Released:** October 28, 2003

**Song Length:** 3:41

**Vocals:** Julian Casablancas

**Guitar:** Albert Hammond Jr.

**Bass:** Nikolai Fraiture

**Drums:** Fabrizio Moretti

| DEVELOPER'S TOP SCORES | |
|---|---|
| Bass | 140,825 |
| Drums | 202,400 |
| Guitar | 2,915,551 |
| Vocals | 11,415,889 |
| Band | 16,082,750 |

Strokes singer Julian Casablancas, guitarist Nick Valensi, and drummer Fabrizio Moretti all met while attending the Dwight School in uptown Manhattan

## REHEARSAL

| Difficulty Ranking | | | | |
|---|---|---|---|---|
| Difficulty | Drums | Bass | Guitar | Vocals |
| Medium | ★★★ | ★ | ★★ | ★★★ |
| Hard | ★★★ | ★ | ★★ | ★★★ |

## GUITAR

**Solo:** Yes
**Medium:** Select Guitar Solo to practice blue to green progressions.
**Hard:** Play Chorus 1 through the Guitar Solo A to discover how much command you have over the entire fret board.

## DRUMS

**Medium:** A nice tutorial on basic drum beats. Master the song and you'll be ready to tackle harder material.
**Hard:** Practice Chorus 1 until you can nail the kick and red snare notes consistently.

## VOCALS

**Percussion:** Yes
**Notes:** You'll need to have range to pull off this one. Just remember to enter overdrive when you see your Crowd meter steadily declining.

## BASS

**Medium:** Having trouble with rapid strumming? This song will test your stamina and hone your consistency in hitting long strings of consecutive notes.
**Hard:** If you need to work on your progressions, practice the chorus—it'll take you from green to orange and back again.

## BAND AID

Feel free to mix it up on Medium difficulty; maybe give the bassist a chance with the sticks. However, if playing on Hard, make sure your best drummer is on the throne. If the singer's range is in question, Medium is a safe bet.

# "RUN TO THE HILLS"— AS MADE FAMOUS BY IRON MAIDEN *

## DETAILS ON THE CLASSIC

**Album:** The Number of the Beast

**Released:** March 29, 1982

**Song Length:** 3:52

**Vocals:** Bruce Dickinson

**Guitar:** Dave Murray, Adrian Smith

**Bass:** Steve Harris

**Drums:** Clive Burr

| DEVELOPER'S TOP SCORES | |
|---|---|
| Bass | 206,491 |
| Drums | 424,129 |
| Guitar | 283,244 |
| Vocals | 13,534,687 |
| Band | 10,474,202 |

**NOTE**

Iron Maiden vocalist Bruce Dickinson is also a licensed commercial airline pilot.

**NOTE**

Iron Maiden's beloved zombie/mummy creature mascot is named "Eddie."

BIG ROCK ENDING!

REHEARSAL

| Difficulty Ranking | | | | |
|---|---|---|---|---|
| Difficulty | Drums | Bass | Guitar | Vocals |
| Medium | ★★★ | ★ | ★★ | ★★★★★ |
| Hard | ★★★ | ★ | ★★ | |

## GUITAR

**Solo:** Yes

**Medium:** There's nothing here a journeyman guitarist can't handle. Play through Chorus 1 and the Guitar Solo just in case.

**Hard:** The song's difficulty steps up quite a bit if you're used to playing it on Medium. Select Verse 1 for chord transitions and the entire Bridge for even faster transitions.

After the Intro, you can pretty much strum up and down constantly without dropping a note. The only exception is during the chorus when there is a short sustained note.

## DRUMS

**Medium:** This is a unique galloping drum beat that is tough to pick up at first. Use both hands to play the stream of yellow notes that appear during the intro.

**Hard:** Only experienced drummers should attempt this difficulty level. The tempo is way too fast, and the sheer number of notes is simply daunting.

During the verses, hit both the yellow notes that appear after each kick drum with one strike from the stick. When you hit the drum pad, let the stick vibrate in your hand to strike the pad twice.

## VOCALS

**Percussion:** No

**Notes:** Bruce has got some range and some lungs! If you don't have fun singing this one, check for a pulse. Use the talking parts as a crutch to pick you back up.

## BASS

**Medium:** This song is a really long seminar on continuous notes, but the Bridge is a nice exercise in increasing your speed and accuracy.

**Hard:** A bit more up-tempo than if played on Medium, but other than that, the bass line is the same.

Spandex pants, tall socks, and a chain-mail shirt are required when performing this song. Oh, and don't forget to prop one foot on a monitor and raise your hand to the sky! Maiden forever!

# BAND AID

The unique galloping drum line will be a problem for less-than-experienced drummers, no matter the difficulty. It's best to rehearse this song before you attempt it. However, if your drummer has played it before, then any experienced bassist and guitarist can succeed with their respective instruments.

111

# "SABOTAGE"—BEASTIE BOYS

## BACKGROUND

**Album:** III Communication

**Released:** May 23, 1994

**Song Length:** 2:58

**Vocals:** Adam "Adrock" Horovitz, Michael "Mike D" Diamond, Adam "MCA" Yaunch

**Guitar:** Adam "Adrock" Horovitz

**Bass:** Adam "MCA" Yaunch

**Drums:** Michael "Mike D" Diamond

| DEVELOPER'S TOP SCORES ||
|---|---|
| Bass | 231,289 |
| Drums | 109,925 |
| Guitar | 2,847,340 |
| Vocals | 4,453,714 |
| Band | 9,112,358 |

The Brooklyn-based Beastie Boys started out as a hardcore punk band.

Reportedly, "Beastie" is an acronym that stands for "Boys Entering Anarchistic States Toward Internal Excellence."

## REHEARSAL

| Difficulty Ranking |||||
|---|---|---|---|---|
| Difficulty | Drums | Bass | Guitar | Vocals |
| Medium | ★★ | ★ | ★★★ | ★★ |
| Hard | ★ | ★★★ | ★★ | |

# GUITAR

**Solo:** No

**Medium:** Select Scratch Break 1 to practice some interesting transitions.

**Hard:** Scratch Break 1 will test your ability to play green/red chords; then quickly move down the fret board to pick up yellow, blue, and orange notes and chords. Some are hammer-on notes, though, so you should be able to pick up the transitions.

# DRUMS

**Medium:** Basic beats; nothing you haven't played before.

**Hard:** Practice the bridge to get the hang of hitting the yellow and red notes, and then add the kick drum when you're comfortable keeping the beat.

An aspiring rock star should twirl his sticks in the air near the end of the bass riff, but a true rock star would do it in between every blue/red combo during the buildup!

# VOCALS

**Percussion:** No

**Notes:** All talking and no notes, so as long as you begin and end the phrases on time, and keep up with most of the words, you'll be fine.

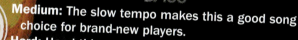

# BASS

**Medium:** The slow tempo makes this a good song choice for brand-new players.

**Hard:** Hand this over to anyone who says playing bass is easy. Get through this and you're officially an experienced bassist.

On Hard difficulty, during the long series of orange and yellow notes, the orange notes are hammer-ons, so shift your hand down the fret board and don't overstrum.

# BAND AID

Can't hold a note? This is the song for you. And rejoice, bassists, finally a bass line that trumps the guitar line! Pull it off on Hard and then wink at the guitarist's groupie.

# "SAY IT AIN'T SO"—WEEZER

## BACKGROUND

**Album:** Weezer (Blue Album)

**Released:** 1995

**Song Length:** 4:18

**Vocals:** Rivers Cuomo

**Guitar:** Rivers Cuomo, Brian Bell

**Bass:** Matt Sharp

**Drums:** Patrick Wilson

| DEVELOPER'S TOP SCORES | |
|---|---|
| Bass | 69,752 |
| Drums | 160,880 |
| Guitar | 2,034,649 |
| Vocals | 13,838,023 |
| Band | 6,433,022 |

Weezer's self-titled debut, referred to as *The Blue Album* because of its blue cover, was produced by former Cars' lead singer Ric Ocasek.

Weezer played their first gig in L.A. opening for Dogstar, a band featuring Keanu Reeves on bass.

## REHEARSAL

| Difficulty Ranking | | | | |
|---|---|---|---|---|
| Difficulty | Drums | Bass | Guitar | Vocals |
| Medium | ★★ | ★ | ★★★ | ↗ |
| Hard | ★★ | ★ | ★★★ | |

## GUITAR

**Medium:** Practice Chorus 3 for basic chord transitions.

**Hard:** Select the chorus for harder chord transitions. Remember to shift your index finger when moving from green/yellow to yellow/orange.

## DRUMS

**Medium:** Practice Verse 1 and Verse 1A—they are variations of a common rhythm.

**Hard:** Practice the chorus to nail the extra kick drum. Also, practice moving from green/kick to red/yellow.

## VOCALS

**Percussion:** Yes

**Notes:** This is a dynamic and fun song for budding singers. It features highs, lows, and even a staccato verse.

## BASS

**Medium:** Very basic, but the end of the bridge might give a novice some problems.

**Hard:** Practice the verses, as you must transition from blue to orange and then back to yellow.

# BAND AID

Put your most inexperienced player on the bass. A drummer who is comfortable counting and executing basic beats will have no problem keeping up on either difficulty. Get a guitarist who is apt at chord transitions.

# "SEVEN"—VAGIANT

## BACKGROUND

**Album:** Public Display of Infection

**Released:** 2007

**Length:** 2:30

**Vocals:** The Hellion

**Guitar:** The Hellion, Elena Siegman

**Bass:** Leeanne Williams

**Drummer:** LoWreck

| DEVELOPER'S TOP SCORES | |
|---|---|
| Bass | — |
| Drums | 234,240 |
| Guitar | 435,518 |
| Vocals | 16,302,727 |
| Band | 1,333,146 |

Pronunciation tip: Vagiant rhymes with "defiant." Sort of.

The Hellion, singer and guitarist for Vagiant, plays on the Durotan server. The rest of the band makes fun of her for it.

## REHEARSAL

| Difficulty Ranking | | | | |
|---|---|---|---|---|
| Difficulty | Drums | Bass | Guitar | Vocals |
| Medium | ★★★ | ★ | ★★ | ★★★★ |
| Hard | ★★★ | ★ | ★★ | |

## GUITAR

**Solo:** No

**Medium:** If you find that playing the red/blue chord with your middle finger and pinky during the bridge is uncomfortable, shift your index finger to the red fret.

**Hard:** Play through the bridge and you'll understand the importance of keeping your finger pressed on the lower note. It's also a good exercise in shifting your hand down the fret board to grab those blue/orange chords.

## DRUMS

**Medium:** While keeping the beat with the kick drum, a true drummer stands up during the chorus break and claps his hands.

**Hard:** This song offers very little challenge for an experienced drummer, but the transition at the end of the bridge is worth nailing.

## VOCALS

**Percussion:** No

**Notes:** If you're a guy, this is quite possibly the most romantic song ever written. Ever. Period. Let the women have Sade and Celine; we want Vagiant! Place your relaxed vocal style on the chopping block and bust out with some angst or face the Hellion's wrath.

## BASS

**Medium:** The bridge contains several single notes followed by sustained notes of the same color, a brief respite from the onslaught of consecutive notes.

**Hard:** Get used to strumming up *and* down or this song will humble you. Try the bridge and hit the long string of orange notes.

## BAND AID

This song will pose no problem for players who have a little bit of experience on their chosen instruments and know how to strum and drum quickly. However, only experienced vocalists need apply.

# "SHOULD I STAY OR SHOULD I GO"—THE CLASH

## BACKGROUND

**Album:** Combat Rock

**Released:** June 10, 1982

**Song Length:** 3:06

**Vocals:** Joe Strummer

**Guitar:** Mick Jones (Lead), Joe Strummer (Rhythm)

**Bass:** Paul Simonon

**Drums:** Topper Headon

| DEVELOPER'S TOP SCORES | |
| --- | --- |
| Bass | 57,347 |
| Drums | 124,325 |
| Guitar | 2,250,469 |
| Vocals | 8,606,467 |
| Band | 1,830,763 |

Despite being left-handed, The Clash's Joe Strummer was taught to play right-handed by the band.

The Clash played their first gig on July 4, 1976, opening for fellow punk progenitors the Sex Pistols.

## REHEARSAL

| Difficulty Ranking | | | | |
| --- | --- | --- | --- | --- |
| Difficulty | Drums | Bass | Guitar | Vocals |
| Medium | ★★★ | ★ | ★★ | ★★ |
| Hard | ★★★ | ★ | ★★ | |

## GUITAR

**Solo:** No
**Medium:** Practice Chorus 3 for some rapid single-to-sustained note progressions.
**Hard:** The song speeds up at the chorus; practice getting through that and you're golden.

During the chorus on Hard difficulty, shift your index finger to the red note. That way your ring finger can keep the blue key pressed and you can simply alternate pressing the red and yellow keys with your index and middle fingers, respectively. Just remember to shift back to home position to hit the green/yellow notes.

## DRUMS

**Medium:** Practice the chorus to work on your consistency.
**Hard:** Select the chorus and see if you can master the quick transition between the red/blue chords and the yellow notes.

## VOCALS

**Percussion:** Yes
**Notes:** A fairly straightforward and even-pitched vocal track.

## BASS

**Medium:** The notes are spaced out—a perfect song for a first-time player.
**Hard:** Practice the chorus to hone your finger progressions. You'll learn to go from red to yellow to blue to orange and then back again.

The progression during the chorus on Hard difficulty is much easier if you shift your index finger to the red note.

# BAND AID

Even a first-time player can keep up with the bass line, and a beginner can handle the axe work. Grab a decent drummer to handle the skins, though. The vocals are pretty straightforward, so don't worry too much about the unseasoned lead singer who's fronting your band.

119

# "SUFFRAGETTE CITY"— DAVID BOWIE

## BACKGROUND

**Album:** The Rise and Fall of Ziggy Stardust and the Spiders from Mars

**Released:** September 1, 1972

**Song Length:** 3:25

**Vocals:** David Bowie

**Guitar:** David Bowie

**Bass:** Trevor Bolder

**Drums:** Mick "Woody" Woodmansey

| DEVELOPER'S TOP SCORES | |
|---|---|
| Bass | 101,784 |
| Drums | 193,175 |
| Guitar | 4,134,736 |
| Vocals | 10,058,599 |
| Band | 1,263,397 |

David Bowie's eyes appear to be different colors, but only because one of his pupils is permanently dilated, due to a childhood injury.

David Bowie is one of music's most esteemed chameleons, having drastically transformed his image and sound many times over the course of his four-decade career.

## REHEARSAL

| Difficulty Ranking | | | | |
|---|---|---|---|---|
| Difficulty | Drums | Bass | Guitar | Vocals |
| Medium | ★★ | ★ | ★★★ | ★★★★★ |
| Hard | ★★ | ★ | ★★★ | |

## GUITAR

**Solo:** Yes
**Medium:** Practice Outro; it has a nasty and quick green to blue to yellow fret transition.
**Hard:** This song earns the Hard difficulty rating and then some. You'll need to run through the song a few times, possibly at a reduced speed, before you can wrap your head around it.

## DRUMS

**Medium:** Standard beat, but beating furiously on the high hat and snare during the Ending is fun!
**Hard:** Practice playing Wam Bam through Ending to increase your ability to strike the drum heads in quick succession.

## VOCALS

**Percussion:** No
**Notes:** This is a tough vocal track, so make sure you nail the talking parts to bail yourself out of trouble.

## BASS

**Medium:** This song features a lot of red to yellow to blue transitions, so practice it if you're having trouble hitting the blue notes.
**Hard:** The tempo is quick, and you'll be using every fret, so practice the choruses to improve your dexterity.

## BAND AID

In this song's case, Hard means hard, so keep that in mind when selecting a difficulty. Even on Medium you'll need a decent group in order to score well.

# "THE HAND THAT FEEDS"— NINE INCH NAILS

## BACKGROUND

**Album:** With Teeth

**Released:** May 3, 2005

**Song Length:** 3:31

**Vocals:** Trent Reznor

**Guitar:** Trent Reznor

**Bass:** Trent Reznor

**Drums:** Jeremy Berman, Gerch on "Drum Fetish"

| DEVELOPER'S TOP SCORES | |
|---|---|
| Bass | 168,142 |
| Drums | 140,120 |
| Guitar | 2,264,032 |
| Vocals | 9,465,589 |
| Band | 1,030,284 |

Though he occasionally involves other musicians, Trent Reznor generally plays all the instruments and produces all the tracks on Nine Inch Nails recordings.

**BIG ROCK ENDING!**

Trent Reznor first worked as a janitor in the sound studio where he recorded his initial tracks for Nine Inch Nails.

## REHEARSAL

| Difficulty Ranking | | | | |
|---|---|---|---|---|
| Difficulty | Drums | Bass | Guitar | Vocals |
| Medium | ★★★ | ★ | ★★ | |
| Hard | ★★ | ★ | ★★★ | ★★ |

## GUITAR

**Solo:** Yes
**Medium:** Play Outro B and practice keeping your finger pressed on the lower notes.
**Hard:** Practice Outro B through Outro C in addition to Break A or this song will give you trouble.

## DRUMS

**Medium:** Break A offers a nice change for those drummers who have the hang of basic drum beats.
**Hard:** Chorus 1 is unique; get the hang of it before you play it with friends.

## VOCALS

**Percussion:** No
**Notes:** All you need to do is last through the synthesizer solo. After that, the vocal track is all talking parts.

## BASS

**Medium:** Beginning bassists should be able to sail through this effortlessly.
**Hard:** Chorus 2 will help anyone who has problems transitioning from green notes to orange notes.

## BAND AID

The bass line on Medium is very simple to play, so hand the four-string to the newbie in your group. Any guitarist or drummer attempting this on Hard should practice it once or twice beforehand, especially the entire break. Feel free to throw an unseasoned singer the mic, as the song's latter half is all spoken.

# ROCKBAND™

# "TIME WE HAD"— MOTHER HIPS

## BACKGROUND

**Album:** Kiss the Crystal Flake

**Released:** April 3, 2007

**Song Length:** 3:06

**Vocals:** Tim Bluhm

**Guitar:** Greg Loiacono

**Bass:** Isaac Parsons

**Drums:** Mike Wofchuck

| DEVELOPER'S TOP SCORES ||
| --- | --- |
| Bass | 130,796 |
| Drums | 185,880 |
| Guitar | 137,390 |
| Vocals | 5,352,436 |
| Band | 2,121,621 |

The Mother Hips formed at Chico State in sunny California in 1991.

The Mother Hips' singer Tim Bluhm has worked as a mountain guide.

## REHEARSAL

| Difficulty Ranking |||||
| --- | --- | --- | --- | --- |
| Difficulty | Drums | Bass | Guitar | Vocals |
| Medium | ★★★ | ★ | ★★ | ★♪ |
| Hard | ★★★ | ★★ | ★ | |

## GUITAR

**Solo:** Yes
**Medium:** Practice Verse 3 through Verse 4 to work on using that pinky finger to strike the blue notes and on strumming a consistent and long set of notes.
**Hard:** Master Chorus 1 through Verse 3 and you're home free.

Green notes are few and far between, so start the song with your index finger on the red fret.

## DRUMS

**Medium:** A repetitive and standard drum beat. Practice the chorus until you get the hang of it.
**Hard:** A seasoned drummer should have no trouble picking up the repetitive beat. Practice the bridge through Chorus 3, as it's a representative portion of the entire song.

## VOCALS

**Percussion:** No
**Notes:** The chorus is on the upper end of the note track, which may cause problems, so make up for it during the verses.

## BASS

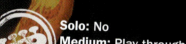

**Solo:** No
**Medium:** Play through the chorus a couple of times to get used to the tempo.
**Hard:** This is a challenging bass line to perfect. Practice the intro through Verse 2, especially if you need to work on your hammer-ons and pull-offs or if you have trouble hitting the red/orange power chord.

# BAND AID

On Hard difficulty, put a competent player on the bass. The drumming and axe work should not be too difficult for seasoned players on either difficulty.

# "TIMMY AND THE LORDS OF THE UNDERWORLD"— TIMMY AND THE LORDS OF THE UNDERWORLD

| DEVELOPER'S TOP SCORES | |
|---|---|
| Bass | 64,653 |
| Drums | 74,467 |
| Guitar | 143,680 |
| Vocals | 6,336,001 |
| Band | 670,941 |

From now on, "Timmy!" is the correct response from the rest of the band when any member flubs a solo, fails out, trips over a monitor onstage, or otherwise embarrasses him or herself. And the last person to call "Timmy" buys a round.

## REHEARSAL

| Difficulty Ranking | | | | |
|---|---|---|---|---|
| Difficulty | Drums | Bass | Guitar | Vocals |
| Medium | ★★★ | ★ | ★★ | ★★★★★ |
| Hard | ★★ | ★ | ★★★ | |

## GUITAR

**Solo:** Yes

**Medium:** Practice hitting the large blocks of chords in Chorus 1. It helps to shift your hand down one fret (index finger on red) after playing the block of red/greens.

**Hard:** Practice Chorus 1. You'll know when you get there, because it looks like someone threw up candy all over the track. If you slow it down, though, you'll be able to discern and perform the pattern.

## DRUMS

**Medium:** While the lack of kick drums (except during the Guitar Solo) doesn't mean this song is easy to play, it does mean it's fun, especially for the coordinately disinclined. And yes, "coordinately" is a word (we looked it up).

**Hard:** It's a pretty straightforward rhythm until you hit the Guitar Solo. Practice that section until you master it.

## VOCALS

**Percussion:** No

**Notes:** You're on your own for this one. Just try not to laugh.

## BASS

**Medium:** Practice Chorus 1 to get the rhythm down.

**Hard:** The Guitar Solo throws some chord progressions at you. Ace 'em or the guitarist will laugh at you.

## BAND AID

The drum line on Medium is perfect for the kick-drum-averse player. An intermediate bassist can tackle Hard, but the same can't be said for an average guitarist. However, if there's one song you can laugh about failing, it's this one, so go ahead and take a chance. After all, if you're performing poorly, the song, like your fame, is short-lived.

# "TOM SAWYER" —
## AS MADE FAMOUS BY RUSH *

| DEVELOPER'S TOP SCORES | |
|---|---|
| Bass | 50,869 |
| Drums | 251,320 |
| Guitar | 172,771 |
| Vocals | 6,728,338 |
| Band | 8,070,977 |

## DETAILS ON THE CLASSIC

**Album:** Moving Pictures

**Released:** January 30, 1981

**Song Length:** 4:33

**Vocals:** Geddy Lee

**Guitar:** Alex Lifeson

**Bass:** Geddy Lee

**Drums:** Neil Peart

Drummer Neil Peart, not frontman Geddy Lee, is the main lyricist for Rush. Apparently he's pretty into Ayn Rand novels and science fiction.

**BIG ROCK ENDING!**

Rush is one of the biggest-selling rock bands ever with a total of 23 gold records and 14 platinum records.

## REHEARSAL

| Difficulty Ranking | | | | |
|---|---|---|---|---|
| Difficulty | Drums | Bass | Guitar | Vocals |
| Medium | ★★★ | ★ | ★★ | ★★★★★ |
| Hard | ★★★ | ★ | ★★ | |

* This is a cover version of a song made famous by the artist indicated.

## GUITAR

**Solo:** Yes
**Medium:** There's a tough part in Guitar Solo C you should practice in order to pull off a flawless solo.
**Hard:** Practice Chorus 1, Synth Break, and the guitar solo.

## DRUMS

**Medium:** It doesn't take a genius to figure out a Neil Peart drum solo would be difficult. Now go practice it until you figure it out.
**Hard:** It's gonna take a lot of practice to get through the first minute of this song, let alone the drum solo. You need fast feet and faster hands.

## VOCALS

**Percussion:** Yes
**Notes:** Pipes like that *and* he plays bass! We're not worthy. Needless to say, high notes are prevalent, so if you begin faltering, kick in the overdrive.

## BASS

**Medium:** Practice Verse 1A and get the hang of those hammer-ons.
**Hard:** Select the entire guitar solo and master the series of pull-offs. You may need to slow it down a bit to get the hang of it.

# BAND AID

Tackle this song on Medium unless you have seasoned and talented players.

# "TRAIN KEPT A ROLLIN'"—
## AS MADE FAMOUS BY AEROSMITH *

## DETAILS ON THE CLASSIC

**Album:** Get Your Wings

**Released:** March 1974

**Song Length:** 5:33

**Vocals:** Steven Tyler

**Guitar:** Dick Wagner, Steve Hunter

**Bass:** Tom Hamilton

**Drums:** Joey Kramer

| DEVELOPER'S TOP SCORES | |
| --- | --- |
| Bass | 183,809 |
| Drums | 254,121 |
| Guitar | 191,997 |
| Vocals | 281,875 |
| Band | 1,319,451 |

Aerosmith played the "Future Villain Band" in the movie version of Sgt. Pepper's Lonely Hearts Club Band.

## BIG ROCK ENDING!

Along with Aerosmith, many bands, including The Yardbirds, Led Zeppelin, Racer X, Motörhead, and Bon Jovi, have all covered "Train Kept a Rollin'."

## REHEARSAL

| Difficulty Ranking | | | | |
| --- | --- | --- | --- | --- |
| Difficulty | Drums | Bass | Guitar | Vocals |
| Medium | ★★ | ★ | ★★★ | ★★★★ |
| Hard | ★ | ★★ | ★★★ | ★★★★ |

## GUITAR

**Solo:** Yes
**Medium:** After the Drum Roll, the tempo speeds up noticeably. Practice Guitar Solos 4 and 5 to see if you can keep pace.
**Hard:** The first two guitar solos are tough but short, so onstage you might be able to fake your way through. However, Guitar Solo 3 is longer, and you'll need to play it well. Furthermore, after the Drum Roll, the tempo increases, so the last two solos are much harder.

## DRUMS

**Medium:** The tempo speeds up considerably after the first Drum Roll, but if you've got the hang of basic beats, you'll stay on track.
**Hard:** This is a great song for an intermediate drummer, and the increased tempo that occurs after the Drum Roll makes it very fun to play.

## VOCALS

**Percussion:** Yes
**Notes:** If you have problems hitting the notes during the chorus, you're in for a tough time, especially at the song's end when it repeats several times.

On Hard, it's much easier to hit the alternating green and yellow notes if you keep your index finger pressed on the green fret. That goes for the alternating green and blue notes as well.

## BASS

**Medium:** The song speeds up a bit after the Drum Roll, but it still isn't too tough, even for a less-experienced player.
**Hard:** The song starts out as fast as it ended on Medium difficulty and then gets faster after the Drum Roll. You'll need to practice Guitar Solo 3.

## BAND AID

An intermediate drummer can take the sticks and handle the song on Hard. The faster tempo that kicks in after the song's first half makes the bass and guitar lines a bit more difficult. If you are a cut above mediocre, you should be able to tackle the harder difficulty level.

# "VASOLINE"— STONE TEMPLE PILOTS

## BACKGROUND

**Album:** Purple

**Released:** June 7, 1994

**Song Length:** 2:56

**Vocals:** Scott Weiland

**Guitar:** Dean DeLeo

**Bass:** Robert DeLeo

**Drums:** Eric Kretz

| DEVELOPER'S TOP SCORES | |
|---|---|
| Bass | 89,813 |
| Drums | 192,920 |
| Guitar | 3,819,520 |
| Vocals | 9,092,062 |
| Band | 1,030,582 |

Stone Temple Pilots had its origins when bassist Robert DeLeo met vocalist Scott Weiland at a concert and discovered they shared many of the same interests... and were dating the same girl.

## REHEARSAL

| Difficulty Ranking | | | | |
|---|---|---|---|---|
| Difficulty | Drums | Bass | Guitar | Vocals |
| Medium | ★★★ | ★ | ★★ | ★★ |
| Hard | ★★★ | ★ | ★★ | ★★ |

## GUITAR

**Solo:** Yes

**Medium:** Practice the verses until you are comfortable performing hammer-ons.

**Hard:** The red to orange hammer-ons during the Intro are tough, as are the hammer-ons during the Guitar Solo. Furthermore, this might be the first time you've had to play a three-note chord (red/yellow/blue). Practice the Bridge through the Guitar Solo to kill two birds with one axe.

Timing is everything. It's easier to execute the hammer-ons if you listen to the song rather than fixate on the screen.

## DRUMS

**Medium:** A basic rhythm with an alternating kick drum.

**Hard:** Slow this down to memorize the high-hat/snare pattern and then add in the kick drum.

## VOCALS

**Percussion:** No

**Notes:** The notes that comprise the chorus are higher pitched, so if you have trouble with those, you'll need to nail the verses and prechorus.

## BASS

**Medium:** Chorus 1 features long streams of continuous notes; practice until none get by the target.

**Hard:** Practice the Main Riffs until you ace the long hammer-on sections.

# BAND AID

Even on Medium difficulty this song can be challenging, so choose the difficulty level accordingly. A weak member will sink the whole band.

# "WANTED DEAD OR ALIVE"— BON JOVI

| DEVELOPER'S TOP SCORES ||
|---|---|
| Bass | 20,799 |
| Drums | 204,840 |
| Guitar | 187,472 |
| Vocals | 14,459,248 |
| Band | 2,797,489 |

## BACKGROUND

**Album:** Slippery When Wet

**Released:** August 18, 1986

**Song Length:** 5:08

**Vocals:** Jon Bon Jovi

**Guitar:** Richie Sambora

**Bass:** Alec John Such

**Drums:** Tico Torres

Bon Jovi guitarist Richie Sambora used to date Cher.

Bon Jovi drummer Tico Torres has played with Miles Davis and Chuck Berry.

## REHEARSAL

| Difficulty Ranking |||||
|---|---|---|---|---|
| Difficulty | Drums | Bass | Guitar | Vocals |
| Medium | ★★ | ★ | ★★★ | ★★✦ |
| Hard | ★★ | ★ | ★★★ |  |

## GUITAR

**Solo:** Yes

**Medium:** This song doesn't speed up until Verse 3, but even then, it won't pose much of a challenge to guitarists with some experience.

**Hard:** Practice Verse 1 and remember to shift your hands up and down the fret board to catch those alternating high and low notes.

If you're weak at playing chords with your middle and pinky fingers, learn to shift your grip on the fret board. Your index finger should move from yellow to red to green. This allows you to use your three strongest fingers to hit the notes.

## DRUMS

**Medium:** Pretty standard stuff, but practice Guitar Solo A through Chorus 3 to familiarize yourself with the beats that are unique to this song.

**Hard:** Practice the Chorus all the way through Chorus 3. If you can keep up with that, you'll have no problem with the rest of the song.

The intro is a good time to grab a drink of water, or better yet, lead the crowd in a slow, above-the-head, two-handed wave.

## VOCALS

**Percussion:** No

**Notes:** There are some long notes in this song, but the familiarity of the tune should see you through.

The Intro is a good time to yell, "I wanna see your lighters in the air!"

## BASS

**Medium:** Challenge yourself and try this song on Hard.

**Hard:** Try Verse 2 and remember to always be conscious of where your index finger is.

## BAND AID

Put your strongest player on the guitar, as the drums and bass are pretty straightforward at either difficulty. It shouldn't be too hard to find a singer familiar with this song, and knowing the tune goes a long way in this game.

# "WAVE OF MUTILATION"— PIXIES

## BACKGROUND

**Album:** Doolittle
**Released:** November 7, 1988
**Song Length:** 2:03
**Vocals:** Black Francis
**Guitar:** Joey Santiago
**Bass:** Kim Deal
**Drums:** David Lovering

### DEVELOPER'S TOP SCORES

| | |
|---|---|
| Bass | 85,859 |
| Drums | 102,000 |
| Guitar | 1,669,933 |
| Vocals | 3,200,374 |
| Band | 1,846,892 |

Pixies frontman Black Francis reportedly found bassist Kim Deal by taking out an ad looking for a bass player who was influenced by both Hüsker Dü and Peter, Paul and Mary.

The first Pixies performance took place at the infamous Rathskeller in Boston, Massachusetts.

## REHEARSAL

### Difficulty Ranking

| Difficulty | Drums | Bass | Guitar | Vocals |
|---|---|---|---|---|
| Medium | ★★★ | ★ | ★★ | ★★♪ |
| Hard | ★★★ | ★ | ★★ | |

## GUITAR

**Solo:** No
**Medium:** Practice Chorus 2 through the ending, and we dare you not to have fun!
**Hard:** Think you have your chord transitions down? Well this song is the test.

Chorus 3 on Medium is a perfect tutorial on shifting your finger position to effectively play power chords.

## DRUMS

**Medium:** Practice Chorus 2 through Chorus 3 and let loose on that snare.
**Hard:** Only confident and apt drummers need apply. Practice the choruses to increase your ability.

## VOCALS

**Percussion:** No
**Notes:** This song is short, but if you have trouble singing the chorus, you're in trouble.

## BASS

**Medium:** This song is too fun to play on Medium—move to Hard instead.
**Hard:** Practice the intro until you nail it.

Bassists, you must play this on Hard, and you *must* bang thy head when the fast snare kicks in during the chorus. Don't let us down!

## BAND AID

Bassists and guitarists should play on Hard—it makes the song much more fun. However, the majority of drummers should stick to Medium. If the singer can handle the chorus, they'll do just fine.

# "WELCOME HOME"— COHEED AND CAMBRIA

| DEVELOPER'S TOP SCORES | |
|---|---|
| Bass | 179,388 |
| Drums | 289,200 |
| Guitar | 4,727,053 |
| Vocals | 21,659,912 |
| Band | 1,642,181 |

## BACKGROUND

**Album:** Good Apollo, I'm Burning Star IV, Volume One: From Fear through the Eyes of Madness

**Released:** September 20, 2005

**Song Length:** 6:14

**Vocals:** Claudio Sanchez, Travis Stever, Michael Todd, Josh Eppard

**Guitar:** Claudio Sanchez, Travis Stever

**Bass:** Michael Todd

**Drums:** Josh Eppard

When Claudio Sanchez was asked to give advice to hopeful rock stars, his response was, "Listen to Maiden."

All of Coheed and Cambria's studio albums to date are segments of an overarching epic saga featuring two characters named Coheed and Cambria.

BIG ROCK ENDING!

## REHEARSAL

| Difficulty Ranking | | | | |
|---|---|---|---|---|
| Difficulty | Drums | Bass | Guitar | Vocals |
| Medium | ★★ | ★ | ★★★ | ★★★★ |
| Hard | ★★ | ★ | ★★★ | |

## GUITAR

**Solo:** Yes

**Medium:** Select Verse 2 to work on basic step-progressions. It'll help you get the feel for using all your fingers. Once you've mastered it, try the intro on Hard for some crazy-fast step-progressions.

**Hard:** It's our belief that everyone has an inner metal demon just waiting to bust free. Well, cancel the exorcist, 'cause this intro will force him right out! Nail it and he might even buy you a drink. Rock on!!

**When the heavy rhythm guitar kicks in during the first verse, it's your band's cue to start head-banging in unison. The crowd eats that stuff up!**

## DRUMS

**Medium:** Practice Intro D, and if you can handle that, you'll play fine through the rest of the song.

**Hard:** The kick-drum timing is the toughest part about playing this song. Practice Verse 1 and Verse 2 to see if you're up to it.

## VOCALS

**Percussion:** No

**Notes:** A tough song to play for a beginner, so hit those energy phrases and save your overdrive until you really need it.

## BASS

**Medium:** Practice Intro D through Verse 1. If you listen to the song, you can memorize the bass line rather easily, thus freeing you up to dance around the stage and score some style points with the crowd.

**Hard:** Although the majority of this song is repetitive, Guitar Solo C and Outro B might cause you to falter.

**During the Outro, get the crowd singing the "oh, oh, oh" with you. And remember, they can always sing louder, but it's up to you to encourage 'em. A simple hand-to-ear gesture or just screaming, "I can't hear you [insert current city name here]!" will do the trick.**

## BAND AID

A great song to showcase a good guitarist, especially at higher difficulties. The bass and drum lines are simple enough to allow a player to attempt a higher difficulty level than he or she is used to.

# "WHEN YOU WERE YOUNG"—THE KILLERS

## BACKGROUND

**Album:** Sam's Town

**Released:** October 2, 2006

**Song Length:** 3:40

**Vocals:** Brandon Flowers

**Guitar:** Dave Keuning

**Bass:** Mark Stoermer

**Drums:** Ronnie Vannucci Jr.

| DEVELOPER'S TOP SCORES ||
|---|---|
| Bass | 186,859 |
| Drums | 144,575 |
| Guitar | 2,316,502 |
| Vocals | 325,000 |
| Band | 972,317 |

While on tour, The Killers' guitarist Dave Keuning was "accidentally" abandoned by his bandmates after stopping at a gas station.

The Killers' bassist Mark Stoermer once had a job transporting human transplant organs as a medical courier.

## REHEARSAL

| Difficulty Ranking |||||
|---|---|---|---|---|
| Difficulty | Drums | Bass | Guitar | Vocals |
| Medium | ★ | ★★ | ★★★ | ★★★ |
| Hard | ★ | ★★ | ★★★ | |

## GUITAR

**Solo:** Yes
**Medium:** Select Verse 2 to rehearse playing long streams of consecutive notes or Chorus 2 for long streams of chords.
**Hard:** Practice Chorus 2 until you get the transition down. You'll need to shift your hand up and down the fret board.

## DRUMS

**Medium:** The chorus throws the red and green notes at you, but they're on the same standard count you are used to.
**Hard:** Practice Guitar Melody 2 and Chorus 3.

## VOCALS

**Percussion:** No
**Notes:** Be ready for the sudden talking parts that quickly turn into notes so you can nail both the spoken words and the transition.

## BASS

**Medium:** Practice this song if you need to work on hitting long strings of continuous notes.
**Hard:** You're gonna be continuously strumming during this song, which makes it ideal for working on your consistency.

## BAND AID

On Hard, you'll need an apt and experienced drummer. Guitar and bass players need to be tireless in their strumming. A singer familiar with the song can easily tackle it on Medium.

# "WON'T GET FOOLED AGAIN"—THE WHO

## DEVELOPER'S TOP SCORES

| | |
|---|---|
| Bass | 250,855 |
| Drums | 557,750 |
| Guitar | 267,899 |
| Vocals | 13,304,314 |
| Band | 2,059,744 |

## BACKGROUND

**Album:** Who's Next

**Released:** July 31, 1971

**Song Length:** 8:32

**Vocals:** Roger Daltrey

**Guitar:** Pete Townshend

**Bass:** John Entwistle

**Drums:** Keith Moon

Audience member Scot Halpin took the stage as drummer for The Who for three songs at a concert in 1973 after drummer Keith Moon passed out midgig.

Keith Moon of The Who is credited with coming up with Led Zeppelin's band name, asserting that the band would go over like a lead zeppelin.

## REHEARSAL

### Difficulty Ranking

| Difficulty | Drums | Bass | Guitar | Vocals |
|---|---|---|---|---|
| Medium | ★★★ | ★ | ★★ | ★★★★ |
| Hard | ★★★ | ★★ | ★ | |

## GUITAR

**Solo:** Yes
**Medium:** This is a good song for a novice guitarist to try.
**Hard:** This is NOT a good song for a novice guitarist. Practice Guitar Riff 2 through Guitar Solo A so you can crush the sections that are all about you.

## DRUMS

**Medium:** The song's length and the number of fills make this a very difficult song to play, even for a drummer who's used to playing on Medium difficulty.
**Hard:** Only the best of the best should attempt this one. There are so many changes that it seems like multiple songs have been rolled into one. This is the reason we practice.

## VOCALS

**Percussion:** Yes
**Notes:** With all the drum fills and guitar solos, your job will seem relatively easy. But don't be fooled—this is a lengthy song, and you gotta have some stamina to get through it.

## BASS

**Medium:** Don't let the slow start fool ya; this song gets difficult. Practice Jam through Jam C and try to keep up.
**Hard:** If there is one song an experienced bassist should aspire to master, it's this one. Practice it often, and use sections of it to warm up with. Most other songs will seem easy in comparison.

## BAND AID

You need to put your best player on drums or you'll be kicked off the stage before the chorus kicks in! The guitarist, bassist, and singer should select Medium difficulty unless they are well practiced.

# ROCKBAND™

# XBOX LIVE ACHIEVEMENTS

| | Achievement | Points |
|---|---|---|
| | **Breakthrough Act** Unlock a Big Club in Solo Tour on Easy, Medium, Hard or Expert | 10 |
| | **Hot Artist** Unlock a Theater in Solo Tour on Easy, Medium, Hard or Expert | 10 |
| | **Top Artist** Unlock an Arena in Solo Tour on Medium, Hard or Expert | 10 |
| | **String Shredder** Finish Guitar Solo Tour on Easy | 20 |
| | **Fret Ripper** Finish Guitar Solo Tour on Medium | 30 |
| | **Axe Assassin** Finish Guitar Solo Tour on Hard | 40 |
| | **Lord of the Strings** Finish Guitar Solo Tour on Expert | 50 |
| | **Rhythm Rocker** Finish Drum Solo Tour on Easy | 20 |
| | **Groove Technician** Finish Drum Solo Tour on Medium | 30 |
| | **Heavy Hitter** Finish Drum Solo Tour on Hard | 40 |
| | **AN-I-MAL!!!** Finish Drum Solo Tour on Expert | 50 |
| | **Howler** Finish Vocal Solo Tour on Easy | 20 |
| | **Screamer** Finish Vocal Solo Tour on Medium | 30 |
| | **Crooner** Finish Vocal Solo Tour on Hard | 40 |
| | **Virtuoso** Finish Vocal Solo Tour on Expert | 50 |
| | **Got Wheels** Unlock the Van in Band World Tour | 20 |
| | **Open Road** Unlock the Bus in Band World Tour | 20 |
| | **Jet Setter** Unlock the Jet in Band World Tour | 20 |
| | **One Million Fans** Reach 1 million fans in Band World Tour | 10 |
| | **Hall of Fame Inductee** Finish the Hall of Fame Induction in Band World Tour | 100 |
| | **Vinyl Artist** Finish the Endless Setlist in Band World Tour on Medium | 10 |
| | **Gold Artist** Finish the Endless Setlist in Band World Tour on Hard | 20 |
| | **Platinum Artist** Finish the Endless Setlist in Band World Tour on Expert | 25 |
| | **Big In London** Finish the last remaining gig in London (Band World Tour) | 10 |

| | Achievement | Points |
|---|---|---|
| | **Big In Paris** Finish the last remaining gig in Paris (Band World Tour) | 10 |
| | **Big In Amsterdam** Finish the last remaining gig in Amsterdam (Band World Tour) | 10 |
| | **Big In Berlin** Finish the last remaining gig in Berlin (Band World Tour) | 10 |
| | **Big In Stockholm** Finish the last remaining gig in Stockholm (Band World Tour) | 10 |
| | **Big In Rome** Finish the last remaining gig in Rome (Band World Tour) | 10 |
| | **Big In Boston** Finish the last remaining gig in Boston (Band World Tour) | 10 |
| | **Big In NYC** Finish the last remaining gig in New York (Band World Tour) | 10 |
| | **Big In Chicago** Finish the last remaining gig in Chicago (Band World Tour) | 10 |
| | **Big In LA** Finish the last remaining gig in Los Angeles (Band World Tour) | 10 |
| | **Big In Seattle** Finish the last remaining gig in Seattle (Band World Tour) | 10 |
| | **Big In San Francisco** Finish the last remaining gig in San Francisco (Band World Tour) | 10 |
| | **Big In Japan** Finish the last remaining gig in Tokyo (Band World Tour) | 10 |
| | **Big In Sydney** Finish the last remaining gig in Sydney (Band World Tour) | 10 |
| | **Big In Reykjavik** Finish the last remaining gig in Reykjavik (Band World Tour) | 10 |
| | **Big In Rio de Janeiro** Finish the last remaining gig in Rio de Janeiro (Band World Tour) | 10 |
| | **Big In Moscow** Finish the last remaining gig in Moscow (Band World Tour) | 10 |
| | **Tug of War Champ** Win 20 Tug of War ranked matches | 30 |
| | **Tug of War Streak** Win 5 Tug of War ranked matches in a row | 20 |
| | **Score Duel Champ** Win 20 Score Duel ranked matches | 30 |
| | **Score Duel Streak** Win 5 Score Duel ranked matches in a row | 20 |
| | **Killer Performance** Five Star a song on Easy, Medium, Hard or Expert | 10 |
| | **Flawless Groove** Score 100% notes hit as bassist, up-strums only, on Expert | 10 |
| | **Flawless Drumming** Score 100% notes hit as a drummer on Expert | 10 |
| | **Flawless Fretwork** Score 100% notes hit as a guitarist on Expert | 10 |
| | **Flawless Singing** Score a 100% rating as a vocalist on Expert | 10 |
| | **Riding on Coattails** Play with a "Platinum Artist" | 5 |